RIPLEY's SPACE

Believe It or Not!®

RIPLEY PUBLISHING

a Jim Pattison Company

TWISTS

Written by Dr. Mike Goldsmith
Consultant Clint Twist

PUBLISHING

Publisher Anne Marshall

Managing Editor Rebecca Miles
Picture Researcher James Proud
Editors Lisa Regan, Rosie Alexander, Charlotte Howell
Proofreader Judy Barratt
Indexer Hilary Bird

Art Director Sam South
Design Rocket Design (East Anglia) Ltd
Reprographics Juice Creative Ltd, Stephan Davis

www.ripleybooks.com

Contents

TWISTS

Universally Speaking

Space is fascinating, and huge, and complicated. It's full of things you can see, like stars, and satellites, and the Sun. It's even more full of things you can't see, like black holes, and wormholes, and dark energy. Scientists have spent lifetimes trying to make sense of what's out there. How big is the Universe? How did it all begin? Where will it all end?

Found a new word? We will explain it for you.

WHAT'S INSIDE YOUR BOOK?

This book shows you some of space's best bits: shuttles and space stations, planets and probes, meteorites and moons, asteroids and astronauts. Every page is packed with out-of-this world info, with special Ripley's fascinating facts and amazing "Believe It or Not!" stories. Are you ready to read on? 5-4-3-2-1…

It's not enough for some astronauts to go into space in a spaceship: they want to take a walk while they're there! A special protective suit (see page 40) allows EVA (extra-vehicular activity). The longest EVA was done in 2001 by two astronauts who stayed outside the International Space Station (see page 42) for nearly 9 hours.

TWISTS

Danger Zone
ASTEROIDS AND COMETS

Look for the Ripley R to find out even more than you knew before!

Comets are like giant, dirty snowballs. Usually comets are fairly happy orbiting far out at the edge of the Solar System, about four trillion miles from Earth, but sometimes they swoop in toward the Sun, growing tails of gas and dust as they warm up.

If you've ever seen a comet, you probably weren't afraid—after all, it was just a whitish streak in the sky. Don't be fooled, though: comets can kill. In fact, it was probably a comet (or perhaps an asteroid) that wiped out the mighty dinosaurs 65 million years ago. It crashed into the Earth and the dust it threw up froze the planet, which killed the dinosaurs. And it could happen again—to us.

amazing!!

This colossal crater, seen here from space, in Australia's Northern Territory is called Gosses Bluff and is about 2.8 miles wide. It was made by an asteroid or comet about 0.6 miles across that crashed into Earth around 142 million years ago.

ASTEROID

SAY WHAT?

...all rocky body in orbit the Sun. Many asteroids ...ted between the orbits of ...nd Jupiter. These are the ...g blocks of a planet that ...ailed to form there.

In 2000, Comet Hyakutake had a tail 342 million miles long—nearly four times longer than the distance from the Earth to the Sun!

Comets are made of ice, dust, and rocky material that came from the Solar System when it was first created about 4.5 billion years ago.

The center of a comet is called its nucleus.

Ripley's Believe It or Not!®

Who'd have thought it? Read all about some totally out there (but totally true) stories—like the teddies sent into space. Members of Cambridge University space-flight club launched four teds on a weather balloon. The teddies wore suits made of foil, foam, plastic bottles, and tape, which had been designed by schoolchildren to protect their furry friends from the -58°F temperatures.

Learn fab fast facts to go with the cool pictures.

twist it!

A comet or asteroid the size of a city crashed into Mexico's Yucatán Peninsula 65 million years ago.

A comet called Shoemaker-Levy 9 crashed into Jupiter in 1994. It hit the planet on the side that was facing away from Earth, so the impact itself wasn't seen, but huge marks could be seen in Jupiter's atmosphere for several months afterward.

Halley is a comet that reappears every 75.3 years. There are records of its visits that go back to May 25, 240BC.

If you had been around in 1910, when the Earth passed through the tail of a comet, you could have tried some of the anti-comet pills that were on sale. They wouldn't have done you any good, though!

In 1908, a strange explosion flattened 830 sq miles of forest in Siberia. It was probably caused by a comet exploding in the air.

WATCH IT

Do the twist

This book is packed with superb sights from the known Universe. It will teach you amazing things about space, but like all Twists books, it shines a spotlight on things that are unbelievable but true. Turn the pages and find out more...

Twists are all about Believe It or Not: amazing facts, feats, and things that will make you go "Wow!".

Don't forget to look out for the "twist it!" column on some pages. Twist the book to find out more fast facts about the Universe we live in.

HOW BiG?

THE UNIVERSE

Everything that exists is part of the Universe, and that's a big, big, big, place. HUGE! In fact, the distance across the Universe is at least an enormous 600 billion trillion miles. Many scientists think that it's larger than this: it may even go on for ever!

The Universe contains more than a billion trillion stars, yet it is mostly empty space. All the stars and planets and other things we can see only make up about 5 percent of the Universe—the rest is called "dark energy" and "dark matter," and no one knows what they are!

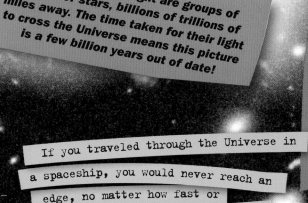

These smudges of light are groups of millions of stars, billions of trillions of miles away. The time taken for their light to cross the Universe means this picture is a few billion years out of date!

If you traveled through the Universe in a spaceship, you would never reach an edge, no matter how fast or far or long you traveled!

The Universe is expanding (getting bigger) every second.

The Universe has no center.

JUST HOW BIG IS 600 BILLION TRILLION MILES? EVEN ON THE PAGE IT'S AN ENORMOUS NUMBER:

How big?

600,000,000,000,000,000,000,000!

seeing stars

Imagine waking up and seeing the stars above you! You don't need to sleep outdoors—artist Rip Read can paint a StarMural on your ceiling. The painting is only visible in the dark, so the "Startist" has to work at night, with the lights out!

twist it!

It is possible that before our Universe existed there was another one, and another one before that, and another before that...

On average, the Universe contains only one atom in every five cubic yards. This is like one cube of sugar in a box with sides over 6,000 miles long.

Even on the clearest, darkest night you can see fewer than 1/100,000,000,000,000,000 (one-one hundred thousand trillionth) of the stars in the Universe.

Three-quarters of the known Universe (that is, other than dark matter and dark energy) is hydrogen.

The temperature of most of the Universe is −454°F, much colder than the coldest freezer on Earth, and only 5 degrees warmer than the coldest possible temperature.

OUT OF THIS WORLD

Ripley's Believe It or Not!®

UP, UP AND AWAY

SpaceShipOne was the first private manned spacecraft in space (exceeding an altitude of 100,000 meters). In 2004 it was successfully launched twice within a two-week period, claiming the Ansari X prize of $10 million. The competition's aim was to boost civilian-led (rather than military-led) spaceflight. The team have joined forces with Virgin Galactic, intending to send customers into space on short trips.

SAY WHAT?

BILLION AND TRILLION

A billion is one thousand million, or 1,000,000,000. A trillion is even bigger; one million million, or 1,000,000,000,000. A billion trillion has 21 zeros on the end!

May the Force be with You

GRAVITY

Gravity, the force that holds you to the ground, also stops the Earth falling apart, keeps the Moon going around the Earth, and the Earth going around the Sun.

The more massive the planet you stand on, the stronger gravity becomes, and the more you weigh. If you could stand on Jupiter you would weigh more than twice as much as on Earth, and on the Sun you would weigh a thundering 2 tons. On the Moon you would weigh so little that you would be a super-Olympian, jumping about four times higher than on Earth. In deep space, far from any star or planet, you would weigh zilch, zero, nothing at all.

floaters!

Everything in the Universe pulls on everything else with the force of gravity—even you and this book are strangely attracted to each other!

Near a black hole (see page 30) the gravity is strong enough to tear you apart.

When you are falling, you don't feel the pull of gravity, which is why astronauts in orbit are weightless, even though the Earth's gravity is nearly as strong in orbit as on the surface of the Earth. The astronauts are in a constant state of falling, but so is their spacecraft, so the astronauts float around inside.

>> space surgery >>

In 2006, surgeons from Bordeaux University carried out an operation under weightless conditions, to practice for surgery in space.

FORCEFUL STUFF

If you could survive the heat in the center of the Earth, you would find that you weighed nothing there and could float around, because the gravity would pull you equally in all directions.

Time slows down where gravity is strong. So, if your parents spent a few decades near a black hole, they could be younger than you when they came home. This also means that people who live on mountains age faster than those living at sea level.

Neurolab was a 1998 space shuttle experiment to test the reactions of living creatures to weightless conditions. It contained 1,500 crickets, 230 swordtail fish, 130 water snails, 150 rats, and 18 pregnant mice.

The gravity on some asteroids (see page 24) is so low you could jump off them.

You weigh more at the Poles and less at the Equator, due partly to the Earth's shape and partly to its spin.

twist it!

Albert Einstein discovered that gravity is a warp (bend) in time and space. Einstein was one of the world's most famous scientists. He lived from 1879 to 1955 and developed the Theory of General Relativity, about how gravity works.

Ripley's Believe It or Not!®

SAY WHAT?

ORBIT
The path of one object around another in space.

Paralympian Wojtek Czyz set a new long jump record in 2008, wearing a prosthetic leg made of space materials! The same material was used in his leg and in a spectrometer to be mounted on the ISS (International Space Station), as both items need to be extremely strong and light.

FASCINATING FACT

Vesta (asteroid) 204 feet

JUMP AROUND>>

Want to break the world high jump record? All you have to do is go to the Moon: our space-neighbor is much less massive than the Earth, which means the pull of gravity there is less, and so is your weight, so you could jump much higher than at home. To really impress the spectators, try jumping on an asteroid like Vesta. Don't forget to take some air with you.

Pluto 79 feet

Moon 30 feet

Mars 15 feet

Earth 8 feet

Hubo Lab

KAIST

SAY HI to a robot Einstein! This US robot can act like a human in certain ways, such as having a conversation, recognizing faces, changing facial expressions, and mimicking emotions.

Home Truths

As far as we know, Earth is the only place in the Universe where life exists. Though we live all over the place, some of our planet isn't too friendly: 71 percent is covered in water, and 97 percent of that water is too salty to drink. Temperatures at the Poles fall as low as −128°F, and in deserts they can rise to a blistering 136°F.

That's just on the surface. Inside the Earth, it gets hotter as you go deeper. It reaches about 10,800°F in the core—about as hot as the surface of the Sun. In the other direction, up in the air, the temperature falls fast and you would freeze to death just a few miles up.

OLD TIMER

Planet Earth is roughly a third of the age of the Universe (making Earth about 4.5 billion years old).

The Earth is carrying you with it round the Sun at 66,500 mph.

251 million years ago, most species (kinds) of living thing died out, including 96 percent of all water species and 70 percent of land species. No one is sure why this happened.

If you traveled back to a time before life existed on Earth, you would be killed by the deadly atmosphere. Without plants, the air would still be unbreathable today.

Ripley's Believe It or Not!®

No one knows exactly how many individual living things there are on Earth, but it is at least 5 million trillion trillion—almost all of which are too small to see without a microscope.

5 MILLION TRILLION TRILLION IS WRITTEN LIKE THIS **5,000,000,000,000,000,000,000,000,000,000** THAT'S A WHOLE LOT OF ZEROS!

...THE EARTH

* Diameter: 7,917 miles (on average)
* Mass: 7 billion trillion tons
* Goes around the Sun in: one year (365.24 days)
* Spins on its axis in: 24 hours
* Made mostly of: iron
* Atmosphere made mostly of: nitrogen

FASCINATING FACT! FASCINATING FACT! FASCINATING FACT!

>>all around the world>>

40-year-old Jason Lewis from Britain was the first man to travel around the world using only muscle power. It took him 13 years to complete the journey on roller blades, bicycle, and a pedal-powered boat on his "Expedition 360."

Photographs taken by satellites and from the International Space Station (ISS) show huge differences in the landscapes around our planet.

If all the ice on the Earth melted, the sea would rise by 330 feet.

The Earth's Poles are about 13 miles closer to the center of the Earth than the Equator.

If you stood on the Earth's Equator, you would be spinning around with the Earth at 1,038 mph.

SAY WHAT?

POLES

The "ends" of a planet, around which it spins.

Our sensational Star

IN THE KNOW...

...THE SUN

* Average distance from Earth: 93 million miles
* Average diameter: 109 times Earth
* Mass: 333,000 times Earth

THE SUN

The Earth seems like a pretty gigantic place, but compared to the Sun it's nothing to brag about. The Sun is literally massive—333,000 times the Earth's mass. This bulk is what makes the Sun shine —deep inside, the pressure is so enormous that nuclear reactions take place, like billions of nuclear weapons going off every second.

The Sun is about one-third as old as the Universe, and about halfway through its life.

Even though the surface of the Sun is much cooler than the core, it's still 10,920°F: so hot that any metal on Earth would melt there. Yet, despite all that, the Sun is a very dull and ordinary star, like many of those in the sky. It is only the fact that it is 250,000 times closer to Earth than the next nearest star that makes it seem so bright.

The Sun sometimes ejects (throws out) plasma. This is called a coronal mass ejection (CME).

If it were not for the Sun, Earth's surface temperature would be about −454°F.

The Earth could fit inside the Sun 1.3 million times!

Shown here is the approximate size of Earth in comparison with the Sun.

HERE COMES THE SUN

If the Sun suddenly vanished, we would see it in the sky for another eight minutes. This is the time it takes for sunlight to reach the Earth.

When the Sun begins to run out of fuel, it will grow so large and hot that it will melt the surface of the Earth.

The element helium was discovered on the Sun before it was found on Earth.

In 840, Emperor Louis of Bavaria died of fright caused by experiencing an eclipse of the Sun.

The Sun gives out enough energy in one second to supply the USA with energy for 50 million years! To produce this, it burns up an incredible 4 million tons of its mass. However, it will take about 5 billion years to burn it all up, so we needn't worry about it running out.

The Sun is 400 times bigger than our Moon but also 400 times farther away from the Earth.

The Sun outweighs the Earth by the same amount as 175 Boeing 747 planes to one person.

twist it!

Ripley's Believe It or Not!®

A pinhead-sized speck of the burning gases from our Sun could kill a man from 100 miles away.

SAY WHAT?

ELEMENT
One of about 100 basic substances from which everything is made.

>>solar power>>

By harnessing the power of the Sun, a family in Montana, USA, spends only $20 a month on their fuel bills. Their aim was to build an environmentally friendly house without spending a fortune; 250 old tires and 13,000 empty soda cans were used in the building!

Blackout

If the Moon moves between the Earth and the Sun, a solar eclipse occurs. Total eclipses are rare, and don't last long—usually less than seven minutes. In 1973 passengers on Concorde flew along with the Moon's moving umbra (shadow) and watched the eclipse for 74 minutes!

Lunar Tunes

It's around 240,000 miles away in space, but the Moon is the Earth's nearest neighbor—although it's as far away from home as humans have managed to get. It is an airless, lifeless ball of rocky mountains and plains of old lava but its effect on the Earth is massive—literally. Together with the Sun, it moves billions of tons of water each day, making the tides that wash every shore.

IN THE KNOW...
...OUR MOON

* Average distance from Earth: 240,000 miles
* Average diameter: 27% Earth
* Mass: 1.2% of Earth
* Length of day: 27 Earth days

There are dozens of seas on the Moon, but no liquid water. The seas are areas of solidified lava (melted rock).

The beginning of the Moon was almost the end of the Earth: about 4.5 billion years ago, a planet-sized object smashed into our newly born world, and fragments from both planets made the Moon. If the object had been a little bigger, you wouldn't be here to read about it.

Ripley's Believe It or Not!®

Because there is no weather on the Moon, astronauts' footprints will survive for decades.

The Moon is getting farther away from you all the time: each full moon is 0.1 inch farther away than the last one.

twist it!

FULL OF MOONS

The far side of the Moon was not seen until 1959, when a spacecraft sent a photo of it back to Earth. The Moon turns as it circles the Earth, always keeping the same face toward us.

In 1968, Russian tortoises flew around the Moon before returning safely to Earth in the Zond 5 spaceship.

The Moon contains mysterious areas called "mascons," which generate gravity strong enough to pull satellites off course.

If something happens "once in a blue moon," it could be more often than you think: a blue moon is the second of two full moons in one month, and occurs about once every 2¾ years. Don't get too excited—the Moon doesn't actually change color!

Wish you were here!

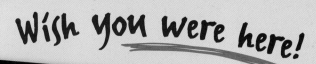

The US has successfully put people on the Moon six times. The first was in 1969 and the last was in 1972. Twelve astronauts have walked on the surface. Neil Armstrong was the first person to set foot on the Moon.

The massive costs involved in putting people on the Moon have prevented further government-funded missions. However, the Google Lunar X Prize offers $20 million to the first privately funded team to land a robotic probe on the Moon.

GLITTER BALL

In 1992 the *Galileo* spacecraft, on its way to Jupiter, took pictures of the Moon using special color filters to record different substances making up the surface. When all the images are put together they give quite a different view—something more like a festive decoration than the Moon we see at night!

GETTING AWAY FROM IT ALL

Dutch architect Hans-Jurgen Rombaut has designed the first hotel intended for the Moon. It is supposed to be finished by 2050 and will have two tall, thin towers, extra-thick walls, and an insulating layer of water to keep out dangerous cosmic rays and regulate the temperature indoors.

Hell Planets

Imagine a world where the Sun is six times brighter than usual, the sky is black, and the weather is hot enough to melt lead during the day and colder than a freezer at night. There is almost no air at all... This is what it is like on Mercury, the closest planet to our Sun.

MERCURY

The largest crater in the Solar System is on Mercury. Called Beethoven, it is 400 miles across.

On Mercury, a day lasts longer than a year.

Ripley's Believe It or Not!®

Seen from some parts of Mercury, the Sun rises twice a day at some times of the year. If you lived there, you the year. If you lived there, you would see the Sun rise about halfway up the sky, then reverse direction and set, before rising again and passing across the sky as usual.

...MERCURY

IN THE KNOW...

* Average distance from Sun: 36 million miles
* Diameter: 38% of Earth
* Mass: 5% of Earth
* Length of year: 88 Earth days
* Length of day: 176 Earth days

The first space probe to visit two planets, *Mariner 10* zoomed past Venus in 1974. It used the gravitational pull of Venus to change its orbit and head off to Mercury. Over 30 years later, *Messenger* has become only the second spacecraft to send back data about Mercury.

IN THE KNOW...
...VENUS

✳ Average distance from Sun: 67 million miles

✳ Diameter: 95% of Earth

✳ Mass: 82% of Earth

✳ Length of year: 225 Earth days

✳ Length of day: 117 Earth days

The highest volcano on Venus is called Maat Mons, and it rises 5 miles above the planet's surface. It is named after the Egyptian goddess of justice and truth. Every surface feature on Venus is named after a female, with just three exceptions.

>> *Messenger* was launched on the night of August 3, 2004. >>

SULPHURIC ACID *Dangerous liquid which "eats away" many materials.*

VENUS

Though farther from the Sun than Mercury, Venus is even hotter (about 860°F), because it is blanketed by a thick atmosphere. Without protection, you would die quickly, and not just from the heat: on Venus the air is deadly. Conditions on Venus are so extreme that no space probe that has managed to land there has survived for more than a few hours.

twist it!

The rain on Venus is made of sulphuric acid, but it boils away before it reaches the ground.

Venus has more dry land than anywhere else in the Solar System.

Venus spins backward, so the Sun rises in the West there—or it would if it were not too cloudy to see it.

On Venus, the sky is orange. On Mercury, it is black.

TOTALLY OUT THERE

SAY WHAT?

Red Planet

MARS

Mars is a harsh world of deserts and dust, red with rusted iron, but it would still win a "most similar planet to Earth" competition, with its icy poles, seasons, and 24.6-hour day. It used to be even more like home, with a thick atmosphere. Rivers once ran across the surface—and maybe living creatures did, too.

Since *Mariner 4* flew past in 1965, over 40 probes have been sent to explore Mars (more than to any other planet), and it is the next destination for human explorers. Despite the thin air on Mars, it does have weather—clouds, frost, and dust-storms—but the last rainy day there was more than a million years ago.

Scientists use 3-D pictures like this one of the North Pole of Mars to work out the amount of water or ice there, and to study the surface and clouds.

MARS

In the 19th century, creatures from Mars were usually called Martials.

On Mars, the sky is pink.

Dust storms on Mars sometimes cover the whole planet.

Viking 1 landed here in 1976 and took photos of the surface of Mars.

In 1997 the first ever "thinking" robot to be sent into space arrived on Mars. The *Pathfinder* rover *Sojourner* was equipped with laser "eyes" and automated programming so it could find its own way across the rocky surface of the planet without bumping into anything. During its travels it sent over 17,000 photos back to scientists on Earth.

Sojourner

Pathfinder

IN THE KNOW...

...MARS

* Average distance from Sun: 142 million miles
* Diameter: 53.2% of Earth
* Mass: 11% of Earth
* Length of year: 687 Earth days
* Length of day: 24.6 hours

• Spirit on the surface of Mars.

Ripley's *Believe It or Not!*®

Scientists are keen to find out about water and ice on Mars as it may hold the key to whether life has existed (or could exist) on the planet. NASA's 2003 rovers, Spirit and Opportunity and 2003 Mars Surface Lab are still exploring the Martian surface and sending back information for the rovers, Spirit and Opportunity, are still exploring the planet. The cost of making and sending these rovers was said to be $820 million for the first 90-day planned mission!

LIFE ON MARS

In 1938, the radio play *War of the Worlds* tricked people in the USA into believing Martians were invading Earth. Thousands of people fled the danger area.

Mars has the deepest canyon and the largest volcano in the Solar System. This volcano, Olympus Mons, is three times higher than Mount Everest and big enough to fit all of Hawaii's volcanic islands inside.

In 1911 a meteorite from Mars killed an Egyptian dog!

Phobos, one of Mars' moons, orbits only 5,827 miles from the planet—that's about 42 times closer than our Moon orbits Earth.

Around 5,000 people (many of them NASA employees) belong to the Mars Society. They practice life on Mars by spending time in remote places, simulating the conditions they would expect on the red planet. Apparently, they wear helmets made from trash can lids and plastic light fixtures!

Twist it!

Planet GIANTS

JUPITER AND SATURN

Jupiter and Saturn are the overweight giants of the Solar System—Jupiter is heavier than all the other planets put together. It has an enormously deep atmosphere full of multicolored storm clouds. It has 63 moons and is surrounded by a system of rings made of millions of pieces of rock.

- Jupiter gives out more heat than it gets from the Sun.
- In 1609, Italian scientist and astronomer Galileo Galilei used his new telescope to discover the four largest of Jupiter's moons.
- Many of Jupiter's moons orbit in the opposite direction to the planet's spin.
- Europa, a moon of Jupiter, is the smoothest world we know, with no hills or valleys.

Jupiter's Red Spot is a hurricane that has lasted for centuries. It is the biggest storm in the Solar System.

The Red Spot is 15,410 miles across—almost twice as wide as Earth. Wind speeds inside the storm reach 270 mph.

Volcanoes on Jupiter's moon Io can throw out hot material at speeds of 0.6 miles per second. That's 20 times faster than the average volcano on Earth.

Io is the most volcanic place in the Solar System.

...IN THE KNOW...

...JUPITER

- Average distance from Sun: 483 million miles
- Average diameter: 10.9 times Earth
- Mass: 318 times Earth
- Length of year: 12 Earth years
- Length of day: 9.9 hours

The Earth could fit inside Saturn 1,321 times over. Like Jupiter, Saturn is shrouded by clouds, and no one knows exactly what lies beneath. It has many moons (about 61) including a weird cloudy moon called Titan, with air like car exhausts and, at least in places, a soft surface with a crispy coating. Saturn is famous for the rocky rings that surround it.

SATURN

Saturn is so light it would float in your bathtub (if you had a bathtub bigger than a planet, that is).

Some of Saturn's rings are kept in place by objects like small moons, called shepherds.

In 1610, Galileo discovered Saturn. His telescope wasn't good enough to see the rings properly and he thought they were moons. The next time he looked, they had disappeared! At a certain angle, the rings are "edge on" and so are hardly visible.

Saturn is about twice as far from the Sun as Jupiter is.

>> double shift >>

In 2008, the Cassini spacecraft completed its four-year mission to explore the Saturn system. It was still in good working order, so it was given a new "Equinox" mission, which will give scientists two more years to make more in-depth studies of Saturn and its rings.

IceWorlds

◉ URANUS, NEPTUNE, AND PLUTO

Neptune is also huge and cold, about −346°F, and the fastest winds in the Solar System (over 1,200 mph). Neptune is blue, with white clouds and the

Uranus is an ice giant. It is so far from the Sun that it is always colder there than the coldest Earth winter: about −328°F. A greenish-blue planet, it spins on its side following a collision (crash) with an unknown object billions of years ago.

NEPTUNE

Triton is Neptune's largest moon. It has active volcanoes, though it is the coldest world we know. The volcanoes are made of nitrogen.

There are places on Uranus where night lasts more than 40 Earth years.

From Neptune, the Sun looks 1,096 times dimmer than it does from Earth.

...NEPTUNE
IN THE KNOW...

* Average distance from Sun: 2,794 million miles
* Average diameter: 3.9 times Earth
* Mass: 17 times Earth
* Length of year: 165 Earth years
* Length of day: 16.1 hours

URANUS

when William Herschel first discovered Uranus, he thought it was a comet.

...URANUS
IN THE KNOW...

* Average distance from Sun: 1,784 million miles
* Average diameter: 4 times Earth
* Mass: 15 times Earth
* Length of year: 84 Earth years
* Length of day: 17.2 hours

FAR OUT

The ice giants are so dim that Uranus was only discovered by accident in 1781.

Neptune, the outermost planet in the Solar System, was tracked down through the effect of its gravity on the way Uranus moved, and not found until 1846.

If you visited either of these planets and looked back toward the Sun, it would simply look like a bright star.

William Herschel wanted to call Uranus "George's Star," in honor of the British king, George III.

Neptune is so far from the Sun that it takes 165 Earth years to make one orbit, so if you were born there, you would not live long enough to celebrate your first birthday.

Neptune has still not been around the Sun once since it was discovered in 1846. It will finally complete its first orbit on June 8, 2011.

If you can't imagine Uranus spinning on its side (rather than like a spinning top, like the other planets) then try to imagine it like a ball rolling along.

twist it!

PLUTO

Pluto used to be called a planet, but is now officially a humble dwarf planet, one of three discovered so far. It usually orbits the Sun outside Neptune and is even colder, and mostly covered with frozen nitrogen gas.

- Pluto spins on its side, in a similar way to Uranus.

- Pluto was the ninth planet of our Solar System until the 2006 discovery of Eris, which forced astronomers to create a new definition of a true planet. The three dwarf planets are Pluto, Eris, and Ceres.

- Pluto's orbit isn't as circular as Neptune's, so although it is usually farther from the Sun, sometimes it changes position! Its orbit crosses inside that of Neptune for about 20 years in every 248.

- The coldest place on Earth (in Antarctica) has an average temperature about four times higher than Pluto's daytime temperature. Brrr!

>> new horizons >>

A spacecraft called *New Horizons* is on its way to Pluto. It was the fastest spacecraft ever launched, traveling at about 10 miles per second soon after it blasted off in 2006. It passed Jupiter in 2007 and is due to reach Pluto in 2015. It will be the first ever spacecraft to study Pluto.

Danger Zone

Comets are like giant, dirty snowballs. Usually comets are fairly happy orbiting far out at the edge of the Solar System, about four trillion miles from Earth, but sometimes they swoop in toward the Sun, growing tails of gas and dust as they warm up.

If you've ever seen a comet, you probably weren't afraid—after all, it was just a whitish streak in the sky. Don't be fooled, though: comets can kill. In fact, it was probably a comet (or perhaps an asteroid) that wiped out the mighty dinosaurs 65 million years ago. It crashed into the Earth and the dust it threw up froze the planet, which killed the dinosaurs. And it could happen again—to us.

SAY WHAT?

ASTEROID

A small rocky body in orbit around the Sun. Many asteroids are located between the orbits of Mars and Jupiter. These are the building blocks of a planet that failed to form there.

In 2000, Comet Hyakutake had a tail 342 million miles long —nearly four times longer than the distance from the Earth to the Sun!

Whooosh...

The center of a comet is called its nucleus.

amazing!!

This colossal crater, seen here from space, in Australia's Northern Territory is called Gosses Bluff and is about 2.8 miles wide. It was made by an asteroid or comet about 0.6 miles across that crashed into Earth around 142 million years ago.

Comets are made of ice, dust, and rocky material that came from the Solar System when it was first created about 4.5 billion years ago.

Ripley's Believe It or Not!®

Most comets have two streaming tails: a blue one made of gas and a white one made of dust.

twist it!

A comet or asteroid the size of a city crashed into Mexico's Yucatan Peninsula 65 million years ago.

A comet called Shoemaker-Levy 9 crashed into Jupiter in 1994. It hit the planet on the side that was facing away from Earth, so the impact itself wasn't seen, but huge marks could be seen in Jupiter's atmosphere for several months afterward.

Halley is a comet that reappears every 75.3 years. There are records of its visits that go back to May 25, 240BC.

If you had been around in 1910, when the Earth passed through the tail of a comet, you could have tried some of the anti-comet pills that were on sale. They wouldn't have done you any good, though!

In 1908, a strange explosion flattened 830 sq miles of forest in Siberia. It was probably caused by a comet exploding in the air.

WATCH IT!

Trash!

SPACE RUBBLE AND JUNK

Building a solar system isn't a tidy job: after gravity pulled together our Sun and the planets, trillions of grains of dust and lumps of rock were left hanging about in space. There is a ring of scattered rubble between Mars and Jupiter called the asteroid belt, and even more rubble beyond Neptune.

There are thousands of pieces of space junk in orbit around Earth. Space junk includes items such as broken satellites, parts of rockets, and even garbage thrown from space staions. There are also around 6,000 artificial satellites.

Most of this rubble keeps itself to itself, but some of it falls through our atmosphere. If it is small enough, it drifts down to Earth and just makes everything a bit dustier. Bigger chunks burn up as meteors (shooting stars), and a few reach the ground as meteorites.

The first TV satellite was launched in 1964 to allow the Tokyo Olympics to be transmitted around the world.

Ripley's Believe It or Not!®

Think you've seen a flying saucer? It could just be the reflection of the Sun off a satellite!

This artist's impression shows all the satellites (drawn larger than actual size) orbiting Earth.

METEORIC!

The *Skylab* space station created a spectacular meteor shower over Australia when it crashed to Earth in 1979.

The oldest man-made debris hurtling around our planet is the US satellite *Vanguard*. It was launched in 1958 and is still up there today.

For centuries, people living in Greenland made their tools out of three large meteorites, which were almost pure iron.

Asteroids were once thought to be fragments of an exploded planet.

About 500 meteorites crash to Earth each year, but only about five of these are found and reported to scientists. So you'll be fairly famous if you find one and hand it in.

Some meteorites began life on the Moon or Mars and were thrown into space by volcanoes before drifting through space to land on Earth.

twist it!

ACTUAL SIZE!

Scientists have only three rock samples from other objects in our Solar System. They are from the Moon, Mars, and this piece of the asteroid Vesta, which fell to Earth as a meteorite.

Mrs Hewlett Hodges from Alabama, USA, has actually been hit by a meteorite! It crashed through her roof, bounced off a radio, and hit her on the hip. Ouch!

>>shooting from the hip>>

TRASH CRASH

The first major collision between two satellites happened in February, 2009, when an old Russian satellite crashed into a working US satellite and created at least 600 more pieces of space junk.

LETHAL CLOTHING

In 1965 the US astronaut Edward White lost a glove while on a space walk from Gemini 4. It remained in orbit for a month, reaching speeds of 17,400 mph, and posed a lethal danger to spacecraft.

PUTTING OUT THE TRASH

The Mir space station threw more than 200 garbage bags into space over ten years. They are all still in orbit.

POW!

Space junk travels extremely fast, which makes it highly dangerous. At a speed of 17,000 mph a tiny speck hitting an astronaut on a space walk would have the same impact as a bullet.

Looking Up

STARS

How many stars do you think you can see in the night sky? A million? A billion? Actually, even on the darkest, clearest night, fewer than 3,000 are visible. This is only a tiny fraction of the mind-numbing total number, which is at least 70 billion trillion—said to be more than all the grains of sand on all the beaches in the world.

Some stars you can see are as big and bright as our Sun—and some are much bigger. Many stars are double, each spinning around the other. Many stars have planets, too. Stars usually last for billions of years—but the more massive they are, the brighter they burn and the shorter they live.

These stars make up one of the most massive star clusters in the Milky Way galaxy.

THIS STAR CLUSTER IS HIDDEN FROM SIGHT BY INTERSTELLAR DUST, BUT CAN BE SEEN WITH INFRARED TELESCOPES.

This is the remains of a supernova explosion (see page 30).

Ripley's Believe It or Not!®

Seeing double

About half of the stars in the Universe exist in pairs. They are called binary stars, and both orbit around the same point.

The red stars are supergiants, and the blue ones are young or newly formed stars.

>> star light, star bright >>

Scientists think that new stars are formed inside nebulae (the plural of a nebula) such as this one. A nebula is a cloud full of dust and gas; when it gets squashed, parts of it get so hot that they become newborn stars.

ORION

CANIS MAJOR

GEMINI

TAURUS

Constellations are groups of stars that, from the Earth, look close to each other. They may really be huge distances apart in space, but they line up to form patterns that have been given names through history.

Orion, or The Hunter, is instantly recognizable by the three central stars making his "belt."

Canis Major, one of Orion's "hunting dogs," contains Sirius, the brightest star in our sky. It is about 25 times brighter than the Sun.

The constellation of **Gemini** is one of the signs of the zodiac. It looks like a pair of twins and can be seen around the world between December and March.

Taurus is also known as The Bull. It contains the Pleiades (say "play-uh-dees") star cluster and is visible between November and February.

twist it

The light from most stars you can see takes decades to get to the Earth, which means you are seeing them as they were before you were born.

Some brown dwarf stars are cooler than burning houses.

The star with the longest name is Shurnarkabtishashutu, which is Arabic for "under the southern horn of the bull."

If the Earth were the size of a marble, the nearest star would be 18,640 miles away.

The largest known star, VY Canis Majoris, is big enough to contain about 100 billion objects the size of the Sun.

STAR TURNS

Celebrities as diverse as Britney Spears, Harrison Ford, Bruce Lee, and even the Clintons and the Bushes have had stars named for them! Scientists give stars a name made up of letters and numbers (such as HD172167) but fans and celebrities themselves can pay to have their name given to a specific star.

Star Death

When the Sun runs out of fuel, it will swell up and melt the Earth's surface—but there's no rush to leave home; it won't happen until about the year 5,000,000,000. Stars more than five times as massive as the Sun explode as supernovas, shining more brightly than a whole galaxy of stars.

Supernovas leave behind shrunken remains, and sometimes those remains are black holes. Why are they black? Because they even suck in light—nothing in the Universe can escape them. Not that you would need to worry about escaping—you'd be torn apart by the strong gravity well before you reached the hole itself.

This jet is lots of high-energy particles being blasted away by the black hole.

* The black hole at the center of this galaxy (called Centaurus A) has a mass one billion times more than our Sun.

* Centaurus A is really two galaxies in collision. It is full of new stars that are forming as a result. Trillions of tons of material from both galaxies is gradually being sucked into the black hole.

* Scientists can study this black hole and galaxy more easily than many others as it is relatively close to the Earth. It is about 14 million light-years from us, which means that the light from Centaurus A takes about 14 million years to reach us. One light-year is about 6 trillion miles.

>> 10 billion+ years in the life of our Sun! >>

5 BILLION YEARS AGO
Nebula shrinks under its own gravity and stars begin to form

PROTOSTAR: temperature rises, nuclear reactions start inside to stabilize star

TODAY
Our Sun provides heat and light to the Earth

GETTING HOTTER
Sun gets brighter and hotter (10% hotter every billion years)

Some of your body was formed in a supernova: to be precise, all the atoms of carbon and oxygen inside you.

A supernova was seen by Chinese astronomers in AD1054. Actually, it exploded in about 4000BC, but the light took 5,000 years to get here.

It is just possible that spinning black holes might allow astronauts in the far future to travel back in time.

A supernova releases more energy over a few months than the Sun will over its entire lifetime.

Supernovas can cause the birth of new stars and planets when their explosions disturb nearby dust clouds.

Supernovas can also be caused by one star dumping material onto a companion star.

twist it!

Ripley's Believe It or Not!®

STARTING SOMETHING

This picture of a supernova remnant was taken by the Hubble Space Telescope (see page 35). It is made up of gas and dust. In a few million years, it could form new planets around a sun-like star, like the beginnings of our Solar System.

YOU DO THE MATH!

After some stars run out of fuel and collapse, what is left of them is a shrunken massive object called a neutron star, where the gravity is so strong that you would weigh over 220,000 million pounds there.

A single spoonful of material from a neutron star would weigh a billion tons on Earth!

Neutron stars are so compressed that they squeeze a tenth of the matter that made up the original giant star (before it imploded) into a ball that is 1.5 billion times smaller.

Some neutron stars send beams of radio waves sweeping through space. If they sweep across the Earth, the radio waves can be detected as short pulses. Neutron stars like this are called pulsars.

SAY WHAT?

ATOMS
Tiny objects, much too small to see. All solids, liquids, and gases are made of them.

5 BILLION YEARS FROM NOW
Sun's core collapses and outer layers spread out

RED GIANT:
Sun swallows up Mercury, Venus, and maybe Earth

PLANETARY NEBULA:
Sun throws off a cloud of gas

WHITE DWARF:
nebula cools and fades

BLACK DWARF:
Sun is no longer visible

Getting Together

Stars are gathered together throughout the Universe in groups called galaxies. Our own one is the Milky Way and it is made of about 300 billion stars (give or take a hundred billion)—so all the stars you can see on the darkest night add up to less than 0.000001 percent (or one-ten-millionth) of the whole thing.

Last century, astronomers noticed something very odd—most other galaxies are hurtling away from ours, and from each other, too. They realized that the whole Universe is getting bigger every second, and that everything in the Universe must have been crunched up together long ago. Very, very long ago (13.7 billion years to be precise), when it all began as a sudden expansion—the Big Bang.

🌀 Our Solar System is perched between two arms of the Milky Way.

🌀 If you counted one star a second and never slept, it would still take you about 3,000 years to count the stars in our galaxy.

🌀 Long ago, most galaxies were blue, because of all the young stars being born in them.

🌀 There are different types of galaxies, named according to their shape. The Milky Way is a spiral galaxy—it's not hard to see why.

NO PLACE LIKE HOME

twist it!

Our Solar System is here.

INTO GALACTIC

The nearest large galaxy to the Milky Way is the Andromeda galaxy: it is so far away that its light takes 2.5 million years to reach us, and it is the furthest thing you can see with your naked eye.

Our galaxy is on a collision course with the Andromeda galaxy; but the galaxies won't meet until after our Sun has died.

You, along with the rest of our galaxy, are being dragged through space at about 1.25 million miles an hour by a mysterious unknown object called the Great Attractor. It's hidden from us by dust clouds.

It takes about 225 million years for our Sun to revolve (move in a circle) once around the center of the galaxy.

The Milky Way looks brighter from the Southern Hemisphere, because the southern part of our planet points roughly toward the star-packed center of our Galaxy. We live out in the suburbs, near the galactic edge, and can look out on the stars around us. If we lived near the center, the sky would be packed with stars, and the starlight would be brighter than the light of the full Moon. But, as there is a massive black hole in those parts, you might not have long to enjoy the view.

the Milky Way

>> what happens next? >>

Most scientists think the expansion will go on for ever, even after the stars have all died and the Universe is cold. They call this the Big Chill. But some scientists think that, in about the year 50,000,000,000, everything will fall apart. First galaxies will be torn apart, then stars, then planets, then you (if you're still around, which is a bit unlikely) and finally atoms: the Big Rip.

BIG BANG FACTS

Astronomers see back to almost the beginning of time when they look at quasars. Quasars are very bright objects (caused by various things falling into supermassive black holes) that can be seen across vast distances. To cross those distances, their light takes nearly as long as the age of the Universe.

The Universe is more than a hundred million times older than the oldest person.

For hundreds of thousands of years after it formed, the Universe was dark.

The Big Bang wasn't an explosion—space was only created when it happened, so there was nowhere for it to explode into!

The most distant objects in the Universe are moving away from us at over 174,000 miles per second.

Most of the atoms in your body are hydrogen, which formed very soon after the Big Bang—so most of you is almost as old as the Universe.

Star Gazing

🌀 TELESCOPES

Telescopes allow astronomers to see objects so far away that their light takes billions of years to reach us. Many telescopes gather light using huge mirrors, which is then focused by a lens. Some of these mirrors are ten million times the size of your pupils, which are what you use to gather light. They can collect light for hours on end (which your eyes can't).

There are also telescopes that detect "light" that we can't see at all—like radio waves, infra-red, ultraviolet, X-rays, and gamma rays. So, if you want to have a good look around outer space, take some advice— use a telescope.

These are the "Pillars of Creation," huge pillars of space dust lit by new stars.

This orange disc is the dying remains of a huge star, which exploded thousands of years ago.

The "Trifid Nebula" is a giant cloud of gas and dust where stars form.

These images were all obtained by the Spitzer Space Telescope.

The top of Mauna Kea (a volcano in Hawaii) is home to 13 telescopes owned and run by astronomers from 11 countries (including Japan, Canada, France, the UK, and the USA). The site has more cloud-free nights than most other suitable places around the world.

This is Mauna Loa, the world's largest volcano.

The most powerful telescopes can see so far away, the light started traveling billions of years ago. They show us galaxies as they looked less than one billion years after the beginning of the Universe.

The largest radio telescope dish in the world is at Arecibo, Puerto Rico. It is 1,000 feet across.

Italian scientist Galileo Galilei built one of the first telescopes in 1609. Within a few nights he had discovered mountains on the Moon, four moons of Jupiter, and hundreds of unknown stars.

The nearest star is about one million times farther from Earth than the nearest planet.

The highest speed in the Universe is the speed of light, which is 186,282 miles per second. It would take over four years to reach the nearest star even at this speed. But don't bother trying to go that fast; the faster you go, the more massive you get, and you would weigh more than the Universe by the time you got close to light speed.

twist it!

Ripley's Believe It or Not!®

The Hubble Space Telescope (HST) orbits the Earth so that its view of the Universe is not interrupted by the atmosphere (like ground-based telescopes). It can see a coin 435 miles away!

SAY WHAT?

PUPIL
The dark hole in the middle of each eye, through which light enters.

STARING INTO SPACE

The Spitzer Space Telescope was launched in 2003 and orbits the Earth, taking infrared pictures to help scientists study how galaxies are formed and develop. Infrared is heat radiation, so the telescope has to be kept cool so that its own heat doesn't interfere with the signals it receives from space.

The Very Large Array (VLA) is an arrangement of 27 large radio telescopes in New Mexico, USA. Each one measures 82 feet across (about the size of a house). They are all mounted on tracks so they can be moved into different positions, but work together to act like one large radio telescope.

VERY LARGE INDEED

Observatories with telescopes inside.

As tall as St Paul's Cathedral in London; higher than the Statue of Liberty!

364 feet tall (including Apollo spacecraft).

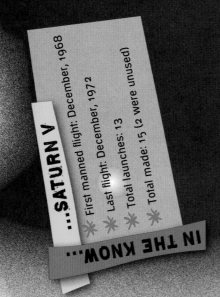

...IN THE KNOW...

...SATURN V

* First manned flight: December, 1968

* Last flight: December, 1972

* Total launches: 13

* Total made: 15 (2 were unused)

The Saturn V rockets used to launch the Apollo craft on their Moon missions were the biggest and most powerful launch vehicles ever used.

Each Saturn V rocket carried enough fuel to fill an Olympic swimming pool, and used it up in 2.5 minutes.

There were three stages in a Saturn V rocket. Each stage separated and fell away after use. The third stage fired twice: to enter orbit and to change its path to head toward the Moon.

Into the Unknown

THE "SPACE RACE"

Looking at the stars, it's hard to imagine what it's like in space. Telescopes allow us to see what's up there in much more detail. But there's nothing like getting up close and personal, and that's what the invention of spaceships has done for humans—and for the various animals that have been blasted into space for research purposes.

The first space orbit was by the Russian artificial satellite, Sputnik, in 1957. The first human in space was also Russian, Yuri Gagarin, who orbited the Earth in 1961. The rivalry between the USA and Russia (then called the Soviet Union) drove both countries on in the "Space Race" to achieve milestones in all areas of space exploration. Many people think that putting man on the Moon, in 1969, made the US the ultimate winners. Nowadays, international cooperation allows us to find out more about our Universe than ever before.

Base has five engines, positioned like the five dots on dice.

33 feet wide.

The 2008 movie *Space Chimps* was based on a true story! Well, perhaps—the main character, Ham III, is the supposed grandson of a real chimp called Ham, who was launched into space in 1961. Ham was sent up in a *Project Mercury* capsule as part of the research needed for human space travel. He landed successfully in the ocean after the flight, and lived until 1983 at North Carolina Zoo.

>> FIRSTS >>

In 1961, Yuri Gagarin (USSR) became the first human being ever in space, and the first to orbit the Earth. The first people to see him upon his return were two Russian farm workers, Anna and Rita Takhtarov, who must have been quite surprised to see him emerge into a field from his landing craft.

Ripley's Believe It or Not!®

The Russian *Soyuz* series of spacecraft first flew in 1966 and is still operating today, carrying astronauts to the International Space Station. *Soyuz* rockets have launched more human spaceflight missions than any other space program.

37

To Boldly Go

EXPLORATION

All modern spaceships are launched from Earth using liquid-fueled rockets. The first of these took off in 1926 and reached a height of just over 39 feet. Impressive? No, but 43 years later, a liquid fuel rocket carried three men 30,000 times farther—to the Moon. The 1960s and 1970s was an era of giant rockets, with giant price tags, and they could be used only once. From the 1980s a less costly vehicle has been used and re-used: the space shuttle.

A space shuttle does exactly what it says—shuttles satellites to space and people to the International Space Station (ISS). Russian Soyuz spacecraft go there, too, and one Soyuz craft is always docked at the ISS just in case an emergency getaway is needed.

The spent fuel tank falls away.

The shuttle lands back on Earth.

The space shuttle blasts off.

External fuel tank

Solid Rocket Booster (SRB)

Cockpit

Orbiter

Atlantis

United States

KEY FACTS

- After launch, the shuttle starts to twist into an arc ready to enter orbit.

- 126 seconds after launch, the thin white rocket boosters are pushed away from the shuttle.

- Next, the brown fuel tank falls away and burns up as it re-enters the Earth's atmosphere.

- When the mission ends, the shuttle orbiter glides back to Earth and lands like an airplane.

The first rocket flight in 1926 was of a liquid-fueled rocket invented by Robert Goddard of Massachusetts, USA. He launched it on his Aunt Effie's farm and after reaching 39¼ feet, it landed in a cabbage field.

HITCHING A RIDE

After landing, the space shuttle orbiter is fastened onto the back of a Boeing 747 plane to be flown back to the launch site, ready for its next mission.

Elevons for control

Engine nozzle

Rudder

In 2009, a bat blasted off on the side of space shuttle *Discovery*'s external tank. No one knows how long it managed to hold on for.

A 1995 space-shuttle launch was delayed by woodpeckers, who pecked holes in its fuel tank.

twist it!

The engine that powers a space shuttle is as powerful as 39 train engines, yet is only one-seventh of the weight. In 25 seconds it can pump enough fuel to fill a swimming pool, and the overall power of a space shuttle at takeoff is equivalent to 16 million horsepower. Despite this, the humble flea can accelerate about 50 times faster.

The fastest humans were the astronauts on the *Apollo 10* mission, who reached 24,791 mph on their way back to Earth in 1969.

Once they're well away from Earth and other large objects, spaceships can keep moving without using any fuel at all.

The first space traveler was a dog called Laika, who was sent into space in 1957.

England's "Astronomer Royal" said in 1956 that "Space travel is utter bilge." The first satellite was launched the following year. How embarrassing!

5-4-3-2-1

Sky Workers

"Backpack" contains breathable oxygen.

Each mission has its own insignia (logo) on a badge.

Jet pack allows astronaut to fly back to International Space Station (ISS) in an emergency.

Inner suit (like underwear) is temperature controlled.

SUITS YOU!

Legs and arms have special suit joints to allow more movement.

Boots have metal rings at the top to alter their size for different astronauts.

Space is a dangerous place: there's no air there, and it's full of deadly radiation. In the sunlight, it's hotter than an oven; in the shadows it's colder than a freezer. An unprotected person would be dead in seconds.

So, to venture into space, people have to be sealed into spacesuits, and the suits have to be warmed, cooled, pressurized, and supplied with fresh air. It's no wonder that a spacesuit takes over six hours to put on, and costs well over a million dollars.

Living in weightless conditions for weeks and months takes its toll on the human body. Astronauts have to exercise every day to keep their muscles strong.

It can be tricky using a toolbox in space—your screwdriver floats away! To help with ordinary maintenance, astronauts use velcro belts to keep their tools on hand, and hook their feet under straps or bars to stop themselves from drifting around.

Astronauts only wear special spacesuits for takeoff and landing, or when they leave the ISS. The rest of the time, they wear normal clothes like shorts and T-shirts.

Astronauts wear this orange suit for launch and landing. It's called an LES: Launch and Entry Suit.

Space Diary

Get up at 6am GMT. We're allowed 90 minutes "post-sleep" to wash, dress, eat breakfast, maybe exercise, and be ready to start work.

DPC (daily planning conference) with ground control center for 15 mins, to confirm the day's actions. My job today is unpacking supplies brought by the shuttle. I think tomorrow will be science experiments, and at the weekend I get time to myself. Will hook up with my family on a video link (until the signal dies!). Most mornings I manage to use the treadmill or the exercise bike, too.

Lunch break is an hour, and the crew all eat together. Warm up my food and take the chance to take photos out of the Service Module windows. Earth looks amazing from up here!

More ground support links in the afternoon to check that all is going to plan. Have to do our chores even up in space! We have a new toilet system for one of the guys to activate, and I need to finish that unpacking. Everything has its proper place!

Finish work at 6pm and unwind over dinner with the others. Time to catch up on some reading, emails, or just gazing at the views. We have movies for the weekends, and tuck ourselves into bed about 9.30 (although sometimes we stay up later!).

It isn't easy using the toilet in space! The waste gets sucked away and put in bags for disposal. On spacewalks, astronauts wear adult diapers as they can be outside the ISS for hours.

When it's bedtime, astronauts climb into sleeping bags, which are fixed to the wall, and hook their arms into restraints to stop them from floating around in their sleep.

Astronauts often wash with a damp cloth to reduce the amount of water used on the ISS.

Food is often warmed in a microwave and eaten from a special tray that stops everything from floating away.

twist it!

Half of all space-travelers get space-sick.

Astronauts grow 2 inches when they are in space, because their backbones are no longer squashed by the Earth's gravity.

The longest spacewalk was in 1992 and took 8 hours and 29 minutes. It was made by shuttle astronauts who were dealing with a faulty satellite.

In 2001, orbiting astronauts took delivery of a pizza! It wasn't delivered by a person on a moped though...

Astronauts can't shed tears in space, so it's an ideal place to peel onions!

If you were an astronaut in orbit, you would see the Sun rise and set 15 times a day, because of your speedy motion around the Earth.

There is no up (and no down) in space.

SPACED OUT

Ripley's Believe It or Not!®

FOR SALE

During a spacewalk to retrieve two broken satellites, American astronaut Dale Gardner had his photo taken offering to sell them to anyone interested! The picture was taken by his fellow astronaut Joseph Allen, who can be seen in the reflection on Gardner's visor.

SPACE AGE

John Glenn was the first American to orbit the Earth, in 1962. He went back into space in 1998 onboard the shuttle Discovery, making him the oldest person (aged 77) to fly in space.

41

Action Stations

It's a long, long, way to the stars: if you were at the wheel of the fastest racing car there is, and if it could drive to the stars, how long do you think it would take to get there? A year? A century? How about 4 million years! That's just to the nearest star—most of the ones you can see are much farther away.

LIFE IN SPACE

The International Space Station (ISS), currently being built 217 miles above the Earth by 16 nations, will be the size of a football field when it is finished.

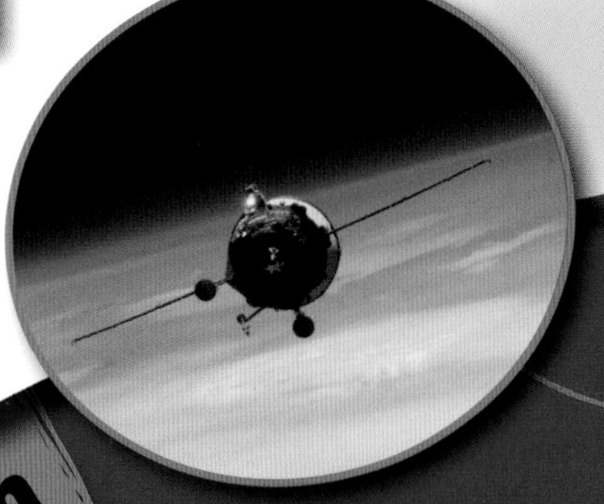

Three to four times a year, the unmanned Progress robot vehicle docks with the ISS to deliver food, water, and fuel, and take away the trash. It burns up as it re-enters Earth's atmosphere. True waste disposal!

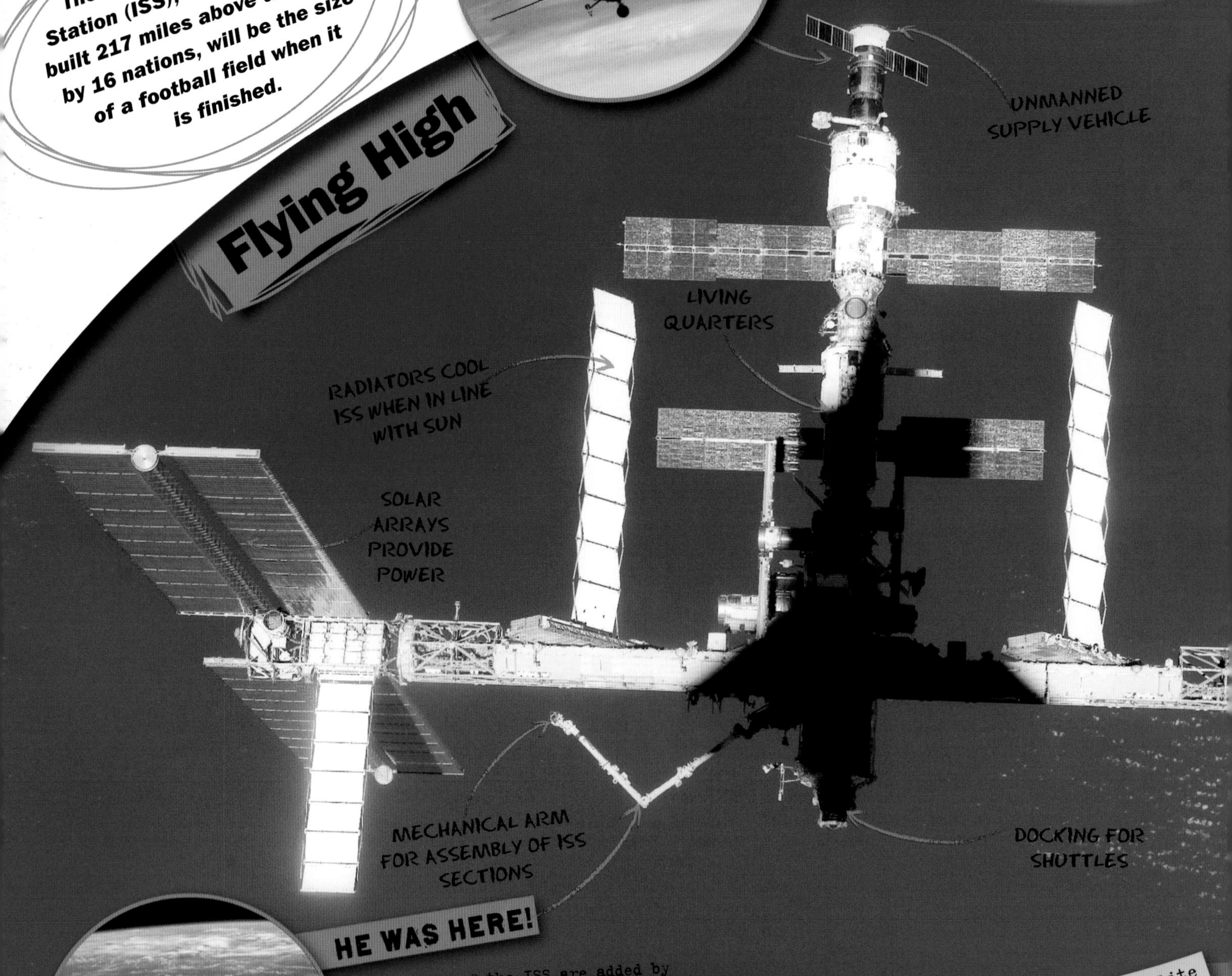

Flying High

UNMANNED SUPPLY VEHICLE

LIVING QUARTERS

RADIATORS COOL ISS WHEN IN LINE WITH SUN

SOLAR ARRAYS PROVIDE POWER

MECHANICAL ARM FOR ASSEMBLY OF ISS SECTIONS

DOCKING FOR SHUTTLES

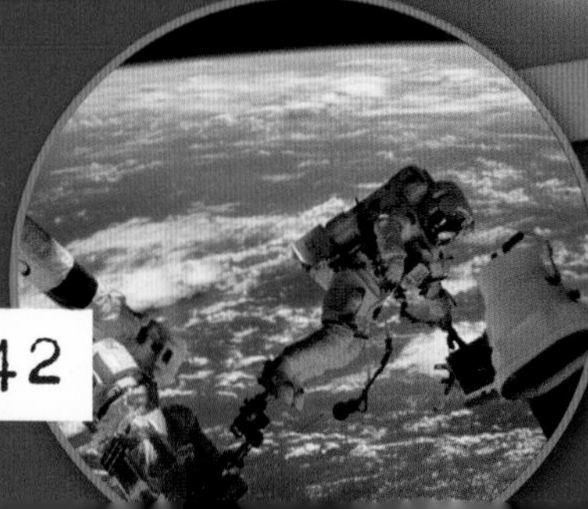

HE WAS HERE!

Extra parts of the ISS are added by astronauts. David Wolf, held in place by a foot restraint on the Canadarm, is attaching a camera to one of the trusses.

The ISS is the largest man-made satellite orbiting the Earth.

However, that doesn't mean people will never reach them. The plans for the first starship have already been made: a spaceship the size of a city, that will fly for a hundred years. In the meantime, astronauts can live in space for months at a time, on the International Space Station (ISS) that is being constructed in space over years and years.

What's this? Believe it or not, it's a photo of London, England, at night, taken from the ISS. The wiggly line around the bottom edge is the highway, and the dark patches just below and left of the central bright section are Hyde Park and Regent's Park.

IN THE KNOW...

...ISS

* Width: approx. 300 feet
* Length: approx. 245 feet
* Mass when finished: 992,000 pounds
* First launch: November 20, 1998
* Number of orbits per day: 15.7
* Traveling speed: 90,880 mph

In a Spin

Two spiders called Arabella and Anita were kept on the *Skylab* space station to study the effect of weightlessness on their ability to spin webs. It obviously took its toll, as the spiders spun uneven webs that weren't as strong as the ones they spun before takeoff.

Ripley's **Believe It or Not!** ®

NO SPACE LIKE HOME

Prior to the ISS, both the USA and Russia had working space stations orbiting the Earth. Skylab (USA) in the 1970s had three crew visits, while Russia's Salyut (1971–82) led to the more successful Mir space station.

In 1869 the first story was published about a space station—made of bricks! It was *The Brick Moon* by Edward Everett Hale.

The longest spaceflight was by the Russian cosmonaut Valeriy Polyakov, who stayed on space station *Mir* for 437 days.

Sections of the ISS are taken into space on board the shuttles *Endeavour*, *Atlantis*, and *Discovery* and the Russian crafts *Proton* and *Soyuz*. The first stages were joined together in orbit in 1998.

FIRST it!

LONG SHOT

In 2006, a golf ball hit by cosmonaut Mikhail Tyurin entered Earth's orbit. It may still be traveling around the Earth even now! If not, it will fall toward Earth and burn up when it enters the atmosphere. It was hit off the ISS from a special tee attached to a platform, and will probably cover a distance of a

FOR REAL?

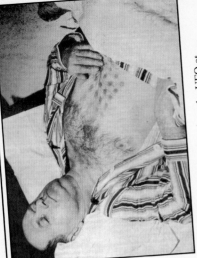

Stephen Michalak said he found a UFO at Falcon Lake, Manitoba, Canada, in 1967. As he got closer he appeared to have been burned with a pattern of dots on his chest.

Aliens are Coming!

● REALLY?

Several specially designed radio messages have been sent out into space, in the hope that someone will answer. So why haven't they? Well, perhaps they have—in 1977 a radio signal was received that no one has been able to explain in any other way—it was so surprising that the scientist who received it wrote "Wow!" on the printout.

Do aliens exist? If so, they might have heard from us by now—radio and TV signals that were broadcast 50 years ago, and are traveling out from the Earth at 983,571,056 feet per second, have already reached more than 130 stars. Roughly 10 percent of those stars are likely to have planets—maybe inhabited ones.

Signs of life

Two Italian professors have found signs of life from outer space! These micro-organisms were discovered concealed inside meteorites, and when put under lab conditions, they began to move and reproduce. Can it be the proof needed for those who believe life exists elsewhere in the Universe?

EXTRA TERRESTRIALS

Launched in 2009 from Cape Canaveral in Florida, the Kepler telescope is on the lookout for planets in other systems. It will spend at least 3-5 years staring at 100,000 stars like Earth section of the Milky Way. It's hoped that it will confirm the existence of sustaining life. that are capable of sustaining life.

Wow!

UFO crash victim!

In 1967, a ticking radio signal from space was detected. The project to explain it was called "LGM" for "Little Green Men." The source turned out to be a type of spinning star called a pulsar.

Some scientists think that there may be thousands of intelligent civilizations in our galaxy.

In 1960, radio messages were sent to two nearby stars in the hope that intelligent aliens might reply.

More than 30 planets have so far been found in orbit around other stars.

Chatting to aliens on a planet going around another star would need a lot of patience. The nearest such planet goes around a star called Epsilon Eridani, and to send a message there and get a reply back would take 21 years.

twist it!

Alien found in Israel!

This weird 5-inch-long "alien" was discovered in northern Israel in 1998. Clearly visible are a head, legs, arms, and fingers—but could it really be an alien being from another world?

erghh!

Claims that this photograph show an alien recovered from a crashed UFO have been put under scrutiny. The crash was said to have taken place in New Mexico in 1950. The picture was sent to Germany for examination and it is believed to be a hoax.

CODED MESSAGE

The two Voyager spacecraft, both on their way to the stars, are carrying golden discs containing messages for any aliens that might encounter them.

The Voyager and Pioneer space probes should eventually reach other stars, after journeys lasting more than 80,000 years. Plenty of time for them to dump into other beings along the way!

Video recording shown as waves

needed to play disc

Shows direction of scan

Diagram of hydrogen atom

Image of record being played

Location of our sun

Space Index

Acknowledgments

COVER (l) © dieter Spears – istockphoto.com, (r) Geoffrey Robinson/Rex Features; **2** Courtesy NASA; **3** (l) © Iuliia Kovalova – fotolia. com, (t/c) Courtesy NASA, (b/c) © Darren Hester – fotolia.com; **4** (c) © Dieter Spears – istockphoto.com; **5** (c) Geoffrey Robinson/Rex Features; **6** (sp) R. Williams (STScI) the Hubble Deep Field Team and NASA; **7** (l) Reuters/Mike Blake, (t/l, t/r, c/l c/r) Rex Features; **8** (t) Courtesy NASA, (b/l) © mario beauregard – fotolia.com, (b/r) Reuters/Ho New; **9** (l) Courtesy of David Hanson, (c) STR/AP/PA Photos, (r) © treenabeena – fotolia.com; **10–11** (c) © suzannmeer – fotolia.com; **10** (l) © icholakov – fotolia.com, (b/l, t/r) Geoeye; **11** (t/l, c, b/r) Geoeye, (t/r) Lewis Whyld/PA Archive/PA Photos; **12** (sp) ESA, (b/r) © suzannmeer – fotolia.com; **13** (c) Courtesy of Yohkoh Project ISAS/Lockheed–Martin Solar and Astrophysics Laboratory/National Astronomical Observatory of Japan/University of Tokyo/NASA, (b/r) © Ekaterina Starshaya – fotolia.com; **14** (sp, b/l) Courtesy NASA; **15** (c/l) Courtesy NASA, (b/r) Courtesy NASA/ JPL–Caltech/Galileo Project, (t/l, t/r, t/b/l, c, t/b/r) Courtesy NASA; **16** NASA/Johns Hopkins University Applied Physics Laboratory/ Carnegie Institution of Washington; **17** (l) Courtesy NASA, (c) Riedrich Saurer/Science Photo Library, (r) Courtesy NASA; **18–19** (sp) Detlev Van Ravensswaay/Science Photo Library; **18** (t/l) NASA; Greg Shirah, SVS, (b/r) Courtesy NASA; **19** (t) NASA/JPL, (r) NASA/JPL– Solar System Visualization Team; **20** (l) A. Simon-Miller/GSFC/NASA/ESA/STScI/Science Photo Library, (r) Copyright Calvin J. Hamilton; **21** (sp) NASA/JPL/Space Science Institute, (r) David Ducros/Science Photo Library; **22** (t) NASA/ESA/L. Sromovsky, U. WISC/STScI/ Science Photo Library, (b) Courtesy NASA; **23** (sp) Chris Butler/Science Photo Library, (b/r) NASA/Kim Shiflett; **24** (l) © Jess Wiberg – istockphoto.com, (r) © Iuliia Kovalova – fotolia.com; **25** (l) © Dennis di Cicco/Corbis, (r) AFP Photo/NASA; **26** (l) © Dragos Constantin – fotolia.com (c, t) ESA; **27** (l) © Bettmann/Corbis, (r) Courtesy NASA; **28** NASA, ESA and A. Schaller (for STScI); **29** (t) NASA/JPL– Caltech/T. Megeath (Harvard-Smithsonian CfA); **30** (sp) X-ray: NASA/CXC/CfA/R.Kraft et al.; Submillimeter: MPIfR/ESO/APEX/A.Weiss et al; Optical: ESO/WFI, (b/l) NASA/JPL–Caltech/B. Brandl (Cornell & University of Leiden), (b/r) NASA/JPL–Caltech/A. Noriega-Crespo (SSC/Caltech), Digital Sky Survey (b/l, b/r) Courtesy of SOHO/[instrument] consortium. SOHO is a project of international cooperation between ESA and NASA; **31** (t/l) NASA, NOAO, ESA, Hubble Heritage Team, M. Meixner (STScI) and T.A Rector (NRAO), (r) NASA, ESA, HEIC and The Hubble Heritage Team (STScI/AURA), (b, l–r) Matt Bobrowsky (CTA INCORPORATED) and NASA, NASA/JPL–Caltech, The Hubble Heritage Team (STScI/AURA/NASA), H. Bond (STScI), R. Ciardullo (PSU), WFPC2, HST, NASA; **32–33** (sp) Mark Garlick/ Science Photo Library; **33** (l) Allan Morton/Dennis Milon/Science Photo Library; **34–35** (dp) NASA/JPL-Caltech/L. Allen (Harvard- Smithsonian CfA), (b) Jean-Charles Cuillandre (CFHT), Hawaiian Starlight, CFHT; **34** (t/l) NASA/JPL–Caltech/P. Morris (NASA Herschel Science Center), (b/l) NASA/JPL–Caltech/J. Rho (SSC/Caltech); **35** (l) NASA/STScI, (r) © Jonathan Larsen – fotolia.com; **36–37** (dp) Courtesy NASA; **37** (l) Courtesy NASA, (r) Rex Features, (b) ESA – S. Corvaja; **38** (sp) © Scott Andrews/Science Faction/Corbis, (l, t, r) Courtesy NASA; **39** (l) Courtesy NASA/Carla Thomas, (t) Courtesy NASA; **40** (l, r) Courtesy NASA; **41** (t/c, t/l, c/l, t/r, b/r, l) Courtesy NASA; **42–43** (sp) Courtesy NASA; **42** (b, t/l) Courtesy NASA; **43** (c) Courtesy NASA, (t/r) Image courtesy of Earth Sciences and Image Analysis Laboratory, NASA Johnson Space Center, ISS Crew, JSC, NASA, (b) © altec5 – fotolia.com; **44** (l) © Snaprender – fotolia. com, (c/l) Mary Evans Picture Library, (c/r) AFP/Getty Images; **45** (t/l) AFP/Getty Images, (l) FPL, (c/l) Courtesy NASA, (c/r) Voyager Project, JPL, NASA, (r) © Darren Hester – fotolia.com

Key: t = top, b = bottom, c = center, l = left, r = right, sp = single page, dp = double page, bgd = background

Every attempt has been made to acknowledge correctly and contact copyright holders and we apologize in advance for any unintentional errors or omissions, which will be corrected in future editions.

RIPLEY's

MIGHTY MACHINES

Believe It or Not!®

RIPLEY
PUBLISHING

a Jim Pattison Company

TWISTS

Written by Ian Graham
Consultant Chris Oxlade

PUBLISHING

Publisher Anne Marshall

Managing Editor Rebecca Miles
Picture Researcher James Proud
Editors Lisa Regan, Rosie Alexander, Charlotte Howell
Proofreader Judy Barratt
Indexer Hilary Bird

Art Director Sam South
Design Rocket Design (East Anglia) Ltd
Reprographics Juice Creative Ltd, Stephan Davis

www.ripleybooks.com

CONTENTS

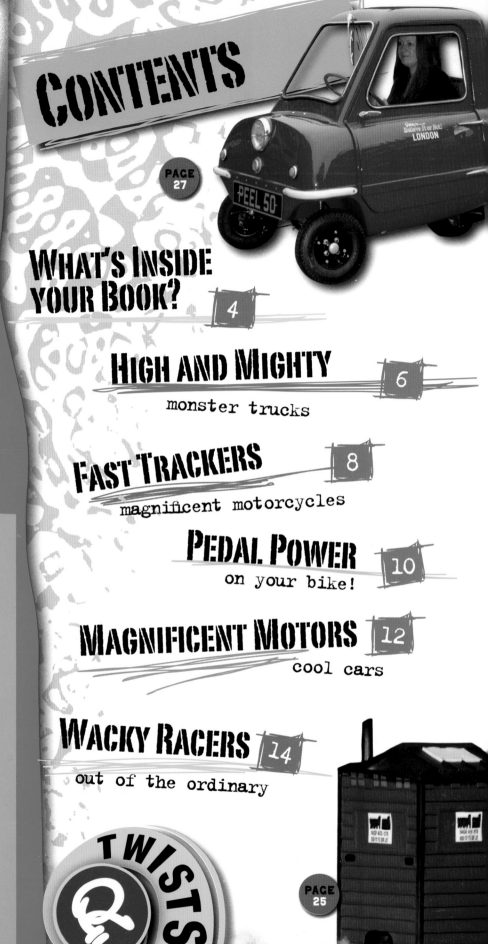

PAGE 27

TWISTS

PAGE 25

MEAN MACHINES

on the move

Take a trip around your favorite mechanical and moving things with this fun but factual book. Learn about the science of flight, put some wind in your sails, and boost your va-va-voom with special Ripley's fascinating facts and amazing "Believe It or Not!" stories from around the world. What are you waiting for? Off you go!

Feeling the need for speed? Wish that your dad's car was bigger than anyone else's? Perhaps robots are more your thing? Humans have invented some mighty machines that let us go faster than ever before, reach other planets, soar through the skies, or simply attract attention from unsuspecting passers-by.

WHAT'S INSIDE YOUR BOOK?

Monster Trucks first became popular in the 1970s. The Monster Truck Racing Association, formed in 1988, set down standard rules about safety and construction. These days, Monster Truck shows make millions of dollars.

Learn fab fast facts to go with the cool pictures.

In 1974 a Monster Truck called Bigfoot (see page 6) was the first Monster Truck to drive over cars and crush them.

Big as they are, Monster Trucks can perform cool stunts such as wheelstands, jumps, and donuts.

TWISTS

Don't forget to look out for the "twist it!" column on some pages. Twist the book to find out more fast facts about mighty machines.

A small boat is fun to sail, but a big racing yacht is one of the most exciting ways to travel. Racing yachts can slice through the waves at 35 mph. Super yachts more than 100 feet long can go even faster. A few of the 50,000 ships that carry goods and materials around the world have been built with sails, too. Using wind power instead of engines saves fuel.

your boat doesn't have n engine, you could roll p your sleeves and row t, or you could hoist a sail and let the wind do the work.

wind power

>> PLAIN SAILING >>

French veterinarian Raphaela Le Gouvello crossed the Indian Ocean on a sailboard just 26 feet long and 4 feet wide. The 3,900-mile journey took 60 days. Raphaela spent eight hours a day at the sail. She has also crossed the Atlantic and Pacific Oceans and the Mediterranean Sea by sailboard.

twist it!

Each mast is 164 ft tall.

The sails are made from a strong synthetic fabric and cover 27,000 square feet.

The ship is 615 feet long, 66 feet wide, and weighs around 16,000 tons.

can carry 308 passengers and has seven decks.

WATER WAYS

Japanese sailor Kenichi Horie spent three months sailing alone across the Pacific Ocean on a yacht made from beer barrels.

British woman Hilary Lister sailed across the English Channel between England and France in August, 2005, even though she could not move her arms or legs. She steered her yacht by sucking and blowing through tubes that operated the rudder and sails.

During a round-the-world voyage in 1997, British yachtsman Tony Bullimore survived for five days underneath his capsized yacht in the icy Southern Ocean until help arrived.

When a Russian yacht lost its rudder in the Southern Ocean in 2005, the crew replaced it with a cabin door.

BIG WORD ALERT!

CAPSIZED

Upturned. A capsized boat is one that has rolled upside-down.

Ripley explains...

Thrust
Low pressure
Sail
Wind direction
High pressure
BOAT

A yacht sail works like an aircraft wing. When a sail fills with air, it forms the same curved shape as a wing. This changes the flow of air to create low pressure. The low pressure pulls the boat along. It can move a yacht in a different direction than the wind by setting the sails at the correct angle.

CLOSE TO THE WIND

The Wind Surf is a cruise liner that can be powered by either computer-controlled sails or engines. Its sails unfurl automatically from the 164-foot-tall masts within two minutes of pushing a button on the ship's bridge. Using only sails, its top speed is about 15 mph, around the same as its maximum speed on engine power.

Even enormous cargo ships can be wind powered. SkySails are huge computer-controlled kites that give extra power and help to save fuel.

Ripley's Believe It or Not!

BRICK BOAT

It took Peter Lange from New Zealand three months to build his 20-foot-long brick boat using 676 bricks. Amazingly, it didn't sink!

Do the twist

This book is packed with amazing mechanical devices. It will teach you cool things about all kinds of machines, but like all Twists books, it shines a spotlight on things that are unbelievable but true. Turn the pages and find out more...

FASCINATING FACT! FASCINATING FACT! FASCINATING FACT!

Look for the Ripley R to find out even more than you knew before!

Twists are all about Believe It or Not: amazing facts, feats, and things that will make you go "Wow!".

Found a new word? Big word alerts will explain it for you.

HIGH AND MIGHTY

monster trucks

They're massive and mean. They leap in the air and flatten cars. No, they're not flying elephants, they're Monster Trucks. These mechanical giants are the stars of stunt-driving shows that never fail to wow the crowds. A roaring 2,000-horsepower engine gives them a top speed of 100 mph.

In the hands of an expert driver, they can spin on the spot, rear up on their back wheels, and jump nearly 26 feet off the ground—but don't get in their way. They weigh more than 4 tons and they can crush a car so that it's as flat as a pancake.

MEET BIGFOOT 5

Bigfoot 5's giant tires were originally made for the US Army for use on an Arctic snow train. The tires ended up in a junkyard where builder Bob Chandler found them and transformed them into Bigfoot 5's weapons of destruction. At 10 feet high, the tires are the largest on any truck. Monster Trucks get to crush about 3,000 junkyard cars in shows every year.

it's home!

Sheikh Hamad Bin Hamdan Al Nahyan, from the United Arab Emirates, is a collector of awesome automobiles, including this towering power wagon, the biggest in the world, complete with air-conditioned bedrooms, living room, bathroom, kitchen, and patio area in the back.

A harness holds the driver safely in the driving seat.

The body is from a 1996 pickup truck.

It has a monster engine of 460 cubic inches.

Each of the wheels weighs more than a ton.

CRAZY

Monster Trucks can jump over 26 feet high and a distance of 130 feet–about the same as 14 cars parked side by side.

If you want to buy your own Monster Truck, it will cost you over $150,000.

It costs roughly $250,000 a year to run a Monster Truck team.

Don't get a flat–a new tire will cost you $2,500.

Monster Trucks are thirsty. They burn 2½ gallons of fuel in each run of about 250 feet. That's 1,000 times faster than a car would burn the same amount of fuel.

TWIST it!

FAST TRACKERS

magnificent motorcycles

Millions of bikers can't be wrong. Two wheels and an engine mean lots of fun. Motorcycles have been around for more than 120 years and they're still as popular as ever. There are motorcycles for riding to work, motorcycles for looking cool, and motorcycles for dirt tracks, motorcycles for racing. They're all different.

The strangest are the motorcycles that are specially made for setting speed records. They look like two-wheeled rockets. On September 26, 2008, Rocky Robinson rode one of these crazy machines, called Ack Attack, at a speed of 360.9 mph. That's nearly twice as fast as a Formula 1 racing car.

power machine!

The Dodge Tomahawk has a huge 8.3-liter engine from a Dodge Viper supercar—that's four or five times bigger than most car engines. The designers think it has a top speed of about 300 mph, but no one has ever been brave enough to try riding it so fast. Only ten Tomahawks have been built and, if you want one, it will cost about $555,000. Even then you won't be able to ride it on public roads.

A BARGAIN, ONLY $555,000!

8.3 liter engine is also used in supercars.

CUTTING EDGE

Why stop at one engine? This motorcycle is powered by no less than 24 chain saw engines. It's over 13 feet long and can reach a top speed of 160 mph.

Dead cool

Gordon Fitch has created a fitting last ride for keen bikers in Britain. They can have their coffin drawn by a Harley Davidson motorcycle.

BIKER BEDLAM

In 2004, Indian magician O.P. Sharma rode a motorcycle down a busy street in the city of Patna with a black bag over his head. Don't try this at home!

German tightrope artist Johann Traber rode a motorcycle on a high-wire 525 feet above the Rhine River in 2003. His father, also called Johann, sat on a trapeze hanging below the bike during the 1,900-foot crossing.

Gregory Frazier of Fort Smith, Montana, has ridden around the world on a motorcycle five times. He's covered nearly 1 million miles.

In 2004, US motorcycle stuntman Robbie Knievel (son of the famous daredevil Evel Knievel) made a spectacular 180-foot jump over two helicopters and five airplanes parked on the deck of the Intrepid Museum, an aircraft-carrier-turned-museum in Manhattan, New York.

twist it!

Engine air intake.

Double wheels front and back spread the massive weight.

Special rim brakes.

SOMETHING'S MISSING

Ben Gulak in Toronto, Canada, sits atop his fast-track invention: Uno, the world's first one-wheeled motorcycle. To give the ride more stability, Ben put the wheels side-by-side just an inch apart and directly under the rider, who accelerates by leaning forward. When the rider leans into a turn, the inside wheel lifts and the outside wheel lowers, so both stay firmly on the ground. What's even more unusual about the bike is that it's all-electric, emitting no fumes.

PEDAL POWER

on your bike!

Bicycles aren't very big or fast, but they are mighty machines. A bike's diamond-shaped frame is so strong that it can carry more than ten times its own weight. It has no engine, but can keep going for thousands of miles—as long as you keep pushing the pedals.

It's sometimes hard enough to ride a bike with two wheels without falling over, but could you balance on just one wheel? Some people actually enjoy riding a one-wheeled, machine called a unicycle. You need a really good sense of balance.

FASCINATING FACT!

Chris Hoy from Scotland is surely the most successful sprint cyclist of all time. By the age of 32, he had accumulated the following titles (among others):
- Four times Olympic Champion
- Olympic Silver
- Olympic Team Sprint Record
- World Record 500 m
- European Champion
- Nine times World Champion
- 27 times World Cup Gold

Built for speed

The best track bikes are built for speed. Their weight is cut down as much as possible, because heavier bikes are harder to get moving. Anything that might stick out, catch the air, and slow the bike down is smoothed out. The bike's body is made in one piece.

The bars are low to make the rider bend forward into the right position for good aerodynamics.

The seat is set high to get maximum power from the legs.

Four or five broad spokes stir up less air than thin wire spokes.

Skinny, low-drag tires.

There are no brakes—they are not needed!

The back wheel is solid, because it slips through the air easily.

PEDAL MEDALS

In 2005, Sam Wakeling rode his unicycle the length of Britain, a distance of 874 miles.

In May, 2007, Quinn Baumberger set out on a nine-month bike journey the length of the Americas, from Alaska to Argentina. He covered 19,014 miles and had 50 flat tires on the way.

The first two-wheeler was built by Baron Karl von Drais in Germany in 1817. It was called a "draisine" after the Baron. There were no pedals. The rider sat astride it and pushed it along with his feet.

In the 1860s, bikes were called boneshakers because their wooden or metal wheels rattled and bumped over rough cobble streets.

A dozen cyclists rode 560 miles across New Zealand's South Island in 15 days on unicycles.

Frenchman Hughes Richard climbed the 747 steps of the Eiffel Tower on a bicycle in just 19 minutes in April, 2002.

Christian Adam of Germany can ride a bicycle backward while playing a violin.

twist it!

It's hard enough to ride a bike in the usual way, but Dutchman Pieter de Hart can ride a bike while sitting on the handlebars and also facing backward! In 2002, he cycled 16.8 miles like this.

THINK SMALL!

Bobby Hunt rides this tiny bike in his stage act. It measures only 3 inches from the middle of the front wheel to the middle of the back wheel, and it's only 8 inches tall.

Wheely fast!

In 2008, Mark Beaumont became the fastest man to ride around the world, taking just 195 days to pedal 18,297 miles and smashing the previous attempt by 81 days.

MAGNIFICENT MOTORS

cool cars

It's hard to imagine our world without cars. There are about 700 million of them worldwide, so it's no wonder the roads get jammed sometimes. A few of these millions of cars are special. They are designed to be very fast, or very small, or just very silly.

Cars have been made in all sorts of surprising shapes and sizes. If you fancy driving a car in the shape of an armchair or a hamburger, the chances are that someone, somewhere, has made a car to make your wish come true.

Awesome

The **Bugatti Veyron** is one of the fastest cars in the world. It has a top speed of more than 250 mph. That's faster than a racing car or an express train.

Ripley explains...

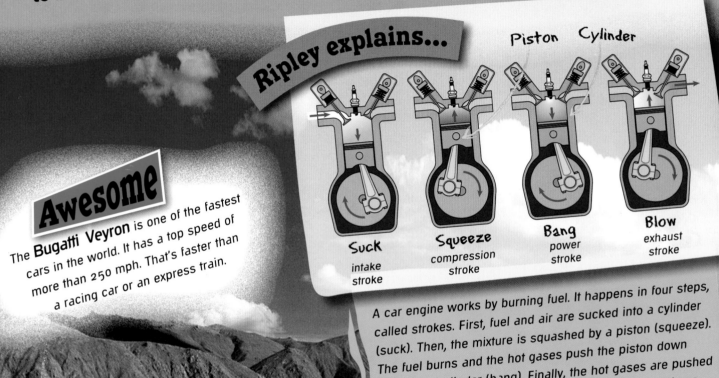

Piston   Cylinder

Suck
intake stroke

Squeeze
compression stroke

Bang
power stroke

Blow
exhaust stroke

A car engine works by burning fuel. It happens in four steps, called strokes. First, fuel and air are sucked into a cylinder (suck). Then, the mixture is squashed by a piston (squeeze). The fuel burns and the hot gases push the piston down inside the cylinder (bang). Finally, the hot gases are pushed out (blow). Then it all happens again, thousands of times every second. This "four-stroke cycle" is sometimes called "suck, squeeze, bang, blow."

twist it!

This couch is no slouch! It can reach a speed of 87 mph, being powered by a 1.3-liter engine. It is steered with a pizza pan!

A single day's consumption of electricity in the USA is enough to power a car more than 36,000 times around the world.

Kenneth L. Moorhouse designed and built a working car only 4 feet 3 inches long and 2 feet 10 inches wide, with a top speed of more than 125 mph.

Edd China invented the "office car," an office desk and chair that can be driven like a car. In 2003, it set out from London, England, on a 1,500-km charity road-trip to the south of France.

The first motor race, from Paris to Rouen in 1894, was won by Count de Dion with an average speed of about 11.6 mph. An athlete can run faster than this!

DIVER DRIVER

Frank Rinderknecht loves to go for a drive... in the sea! His submersible car, called "sQuba," can drive on land or underwater. The car flies through the water at a depth of 33 feet, whilst the driver and passenger breathe compressed air. Instead of a four-stroke combustion engine, the car is powered by electric motors.

transformers!

Brazilian Olisio da Silva and his two sons, Marco and Marcus, have created a real-life transformer. Their Kia Besta van takes just six minutes to morph into a 12-foot-high robot, accompanied by thumping music, smoke, and flashing lights. It took them nine months and $130,000 to create the "SuperRoboCar."

THE CAR'S THE STAR

The Bugatti Veyron is one of the world's most expensive cars. Each one costs about 1.5 million dollars.

The Veyron's engine is in the middle of the car, behind the driver.

The amazing engine is over six times more powerful than a family car engine.

Two pipes on the roof, called snorkels, lead air down into the engine.

When the car reaches a speed of 136 mph, a wing-like spoiler unfolds from the back.

WACKY RACERS

out of the ordinary

Motor racing is amazingly popular. In the USA, seven million fans watch each NASCAR race. Every Formula 1 race has 55 million people glued to their television screens all over the world.

But "ordinary" motor racing just isn't enough for some people. They can't look at a lawn mower or a snowmobile without wondering how fast it can go. It isn't long before they're racing each other. You name it, and someone has raced it. Almost anything can have an engine and wheels bolted on for a race. Beds, barrels, and even toilets have been turned into wacky racing machines.

SUN-POWERED

Odd-looking electric racing cars powered by sunlight take part in the World Solar Challenge—a 3,000-km race across Australia from Darwin to Adelaide.

A large upper surface captures the sunlight.

Solar panels provide power for all sorts of machines, from calculators to the International Space Station. When light strikes a solar panel, it provides the energy to make an electric current flow. The solar panel works like a battery for as long as light falls on it.

The low frontal area reduces energy-sapping drag.

Solar cells change sunlight into electricity to run the electric motors that power the cars.

RACING AROUND

The National Lawn Mower Racing Championships in Mendota, Illinois, started as an April Fool's joke in 1992, but proved so popular that it became an annual event.

The annual Furniture Race in Whitefish, Montana, involves competitors attaching skis to various items of furniture and racing them down the nearby Big Mountain.

Every year, bed-racing enthusiasts flock to Arizona for the annual Oatman Bed Race. The teams push their beds down the main street, make the beds, and then race back to the finish line to the sound of the Chamber Pot Band.

Here's a tale. Emma Crawford was buried on top of Red Mountain, Colorado, in 1891, but her coffin slid down the Canyon in 1929 after heavy rains. Now, as a bizarre form of action replay, every year in nearby Manitou Springs, teams build and race coffins with a living female occupant.

twist it!

These daredevil racers reach 12.5 mph on their motorized beer barrels in Windsor, England.

>> chair-raising! >>

Sixty-four participants took part in the Office Chair World Championships, which took place in Olten, Switzerland. Racers sped downhill over 200 yards, hurtling over ramps and jumps.

BIG WORD ALERT!

NASCAR
A type of motor racing in the USA.

FORMULA 1
A motor-racing championship in single-seat racing cars. Races take place all over the world.

Joel King's jet-powered street luge board can reach 112 mph. The board has no brakes, so he stops by putting his feet down. Ouch!

PRIVATE TRANSPORTERS

just for one

The robot has eyes made of Ping-Pong™ balls.

It can walk at 1.25 mph for up to 6 hours.

Wu Yulu spent a year building the robot, one of 25 robots he has made.

The robot can talk as well as walk.

If you don't have a bicycle, there are lots of other personal transporters that you could use instead. You could hop on a hovercraft that is able to fly, or a tiny plane just big enough for one.

In the coldest parts of the world, with thick snow on the ground, a snowmobile is the best way to get around. There are 3 million snowmobiles worldwide, and some of them can scoot across the snow at more than 60 mph.

Wouldn't it be great to get into a car that in a traffic jam can take off and zoom away in the sky? People have been building flying cars since the 1930s, but you can't buy one—yet.

Sit back and let a robot do the work! This rickshaw is pulled by a robot built by Wu Yulu, a farmer from Mawa Village, near Beijing, in China. Inventor Wu started to build robots in 1986, made from wire, metal, screws, and nails found on garbage heaps. Wu was inspired simply by watching people going past his farm, and by thinking about the mechanics of walking.

This electric engine could change aviation forever. With a battery pack that lets a small, one-person plane fly for about an hour at speeds of up to 130 mph, it could be a giant step toward eco-friendly flying.

Larry Neal has come up with a solution to being caught in traffic. Riding his Super Sky Cycle, you can simply unfold the rotors and take off, leaving the traffic behind you. This personal transporter can take off on a 30-yard strip of road, fly at expressway speeds, land, and then be driven home as a motorcycle, before being parked in a garage.

Traffic buster

Is it a plane or is it a boat? Neither. It's the invention of Rudy Heeman, from Nelson Haven, New Zealand, who has built a hovercraft that, because of its peculiar aerodynamics, is able to fly.

uplifting!

twist it!

In 1992, US brothers Andre, Carl, and Denis Boucher, along with John Outzen, crossed the snow and ice of the North American polar cap, from the Pacific to the Atlantic, on snowmobiles. The 10,250-mile journey took 56 days.

In June, 2006, South African Adriaan Marais and Marinus Du Plessis traveled 13,000 miles by jet ski from Anchorage, Alaska, to Miami, Florida, down the West Coast of the USA and through the Panama Canal.

In 2006, English photographer Roz Gordon traveled the length of Britain, from John O'Groats to Land's End, using 73 different types of transport, including a pogo stick, camel, dog sled, golf cart, and stilts.

In 1949, Molt Taylor from Portland, Oregon, invented the Aerocar, a flying four-wheel car with a removable tail and wings, powered by an aircraft engine.

GETTING ABOUT

Millions of tons of goods and materials are moved around by trucks every year. But you won't see the biggest trucks of all rumbling past your house, because they're far too big for ordinary roads.

Some carry rock out of mines. These massive trucks are the size of a house. They can carry more than 300 tons of rock in one load. Even when they are standing empty, they weigh as much as 190 cars. The massive engine that moves such a heavy machine is as big as 45 car engines and its fuel tank holds enough fuel to fill 20 bathtubs.

In 2004, in Whitehorse, Yukon Territory, a dog managed to put a truck in gear and coast downhill while his owner watched television. A passer-by alerted the police after seeing the truck go by with a dog at the wheel.

06H495   830E   KOMA

Each dump truck can cost $2.5 million.

Fully loaded, a dump truck can weigh 650 tons.

They work in coal, copper, iron, and gold mines all over the world.

KOMATSU

The driver climbs a flight of steps to reach the cab.

Mining dump trucks load up with earth weighing as much as 300 cars.

Each tire measures 13 feet high.

TRAVELING LIGHT

The 2,000-ton space shuttle has its own transporter to move it to the launch pad.

The crawler weighs 2,600 tons and each side can be raised and lowered independently to keep the shuttle level as it moves up to the launch pad. The crawler travels the 3.5 miles from the shuttle depot at a maximum speed of just 1 mph, burning 125 gallons of fuel every mile. The journey takes an average of about five hours.

>> HUMAN HAULER >>

Krishna Gopal Shrivestava pulled a 300-ton boat a distance of 49.2 feet in Calcutta harbor using ropes attached to his teeth.

twist it!

A major road in California had to be closed in 2006 after a truck overturned and spilled 10 tons of cat litter on the road. It took four hours to clean up.

In May, 2006, thieves in Germany stole an entire roller coaster weighing more than 20 tons from the back of a parked truck.

At the 2006 Kentucky Art Car Weekend, Lewis Meyer decorated the front of his Nissan truck with a sea monster made from bottle tops.

British sculptor Douglas White created a palm tree 15 feet 9 inches high from blown-out truck tires in the middle of a rain forest in Belize.

A locksmith from North Platte, Nebraska, made a truck key by looking at an X-ray of the driver, who had swallowed the key. The new key worked first time.

KEEP ON TRUCKIN'

MOVING HOUSE

Ripley's Believe It or Not!®

This house in Palm Beach, Florida, was donated to a charity and moved to its new location by truck and barge. The owners built a new house on the vacant plot of land.

HOME MADE

art cars and bikes

VEHICLE
A car, bus, truck, or other machine for transporting people or cargo.

Some people have to be different. For them, the same car as everyone else just won't do. One popular way to make a car look different is to give it a special paint job. Painted flames, eagle wings, or lightning flashes can turn an ordinary vehicle into an amazing work of art.

Another common way to add a personal touch is to cover a car with... well, whatever you like. Owners have customized their cars and, for that matter, motorcycles, by coating them with everything from postage stamps and coins to fur fabric and cartoon characters.

LADLED WITH LOVE

Chuck Weedman from Beaver Dam, Kentucky, customized his motorcycle by welding on 1,800 ruby red spoons, giving it a lizard-skin appearance.

20

>>FULL OF TASTE>>

Complete with lettuce, salad, and cheese, Harry Sperl's Hamburger Harley Davidson drives around Daytona Beach, Florida. The bike is just one of thousands of hamburger-related items that Harry has in his home, including a giant hamburger waterbed and a hamburger phone. Each one really is something to relish!

mint condition

Ken Burkitt of Niagara Falls, Ontario, Canada, is obsessed with coins, and has covered several cars with them. Each coin he uses is coated with polyurethane, to stop it discoloring or rusting. This MGB Roadster, which is covered in gold-plated English old pennies, is currently on display at the Ripley's Museum in Mexico. Coins are bent into shape so that they mold to every curve of a car.

ROCK 'N' ROLL MOTOR

School teacher Rebecca Bass from Houston, Texas, and her students created this rock 'n' roll motor that depicts many world-famous musicians, including Jimi Hendrix, ZZ Top, Madonna, and Sir Elton John. They covered the car with sculpted Styrofoam, beads, glass, jewelry, and albums.

twist it!

IT'S A COVER UP

One of the exhibits at a stamp fair in Germany was a Volkswagen Beetle car covered with more than half a million postage stamps.

Gene Pool not only covered a whole bus in growing grass but also made himself a grass suit. He watered both daily.

Artist James Robert Ford spent three years covering a Ford Capri with 4,500 toy cars.

Torsten Baubach from Wales covered his Mini with tiger-print fur fabric.

Janette Hanson of Macclesfield, England, altered her Mini Cooper so that it matched her purse.

MUSCLED UP

human-powered machines

A cyclist produces about 200 watts of power by pedaling. This much power could light two or three electric lamps. That's not much, but it's also enough to power a specially designed plane, helicopter, boat, or submarine.

Every two years, human-powered submarines race against each other at the International Submarine Races in the USA. In the air, the most famous pedal-powered plane is the Gossamer Albatross. Bryan Allen flew it from England to France, reaching a top speed of 18 mph.

Amazingly, it's also possible for one strong person to drag a 180-ton airliner along the ground by muscle power alone.

>> DON'T STOP! >>

Bryan Allen pedaled for nearly three hours to power the Gossamer Albatross plane across the sea between England and France on June 12, 1979. It weighs just 44 pounds.

The wings are made from thin plastic film stretched over a plastic frame.

A propeller powers the aircraft through the air.

Pedals turn the propeller.

DEEP THOUGHTS

Students from the University of Quebec, Canada, built a craft that holds the record for the fastest human-powered submarine. Just 15½ feet long, Omer 5 reached 9 mph in 2007. It has a crew of two. One person turns the propeller by pushing pedals and a second person steers the sub. It's a "wet" submarine, which means it is full of water. The crew wears diving gear.

Greg Kolodziejzyk has pure pedal power. In 2006, on a racetrack in California, he cycled a mammoth 646 miles in 24 hours and clocked up the fastest time ever for pedaling 1,000 km—he took just 23 hours 2 minutes. His Critical Power bike is no ordinary two-wheeler. He rides it lying down. It can reach speeds of 62 mph and has a cruising speed of 30 mph on a flat road.

Gamini Wasnatha Kumara pulled a 40-ton railway carriage 82 feet in Colombo, Sri Lanka, in 2001, by means of a rope gripped between his teeth.

PHEW!

Eleven-year-old Bruce Khlebnikov towed a plane with a rope attached to his hair on May 24, 2001, in Moscow, Russia.

In 1909, Walter Flexenberger invented the Sea Cycle, a catamaran powered by a paddlewheel turned by pedaling a bicycle.

In 2000, 20 men pulled a dump truck around a car park in Kenosha, Wisconsin, for an hour, covering a distance of 3 miles.

In 2005, Zhang Xingquan from China not only pulled a family car using his ear, he did it while walking on raw eggs—without breaking them.

In 2006, 72-year-old Chinese grandmother Wang Xiaobei pulled a truck loaded with people for 33 feet—with her teeth!

Twist it!

In Beijing a group of people demonstrate how pedal power can generate electricity that can be stored in portable rechargeable batteries. The batteries are then able to power electrical appliances, such as washing machines.

DID YOU KNOW?

The first submarines were human-powered. In 1620, a Dutchman, Cornelis Drebbel, designed a wooden vehicle covered in leather. It was able to carry 12 rowers and a total of 20 men. Amazingly, the vessel could dive to a depth of 16 feet and travel 6 miles. The crew turned the propeller by hand.

CRAZY TRANSPORT

far out!

If you're bored with traveling in the usual ways, there are some more exciting ways to get around.

Those of you who are really brave could try being fired out of a circus cannon. You could fly 148 feet through the air at up to 50 mph. Or take a leaf out of Felix Baumgartner's book. In 2003, he strapped a 6-foot wing to his back and jumped out of a plane. He glided 22 miles from England to France across the English Channel. You could try fitting rockets to a car, or a jet engine to a boat. Jet-powered racing boats, called hydroplanes, can reach speeds of more than 220 mph.

LED

In-suit drink bag.

Oxygen and temperature controls.

The SAFER pack attaches to the bottom of a normal space backpack.

>>UP, UP, AND AWAY>>

NASA insists that astronauts from the space shuttle or International Space Station wear a SAFER jet pack for spacewalks. If they drift away from the spacecraft, they can use it to fly back to safety. Crazily they fly through space, miles from Earth.

FASCINATING FACT! FASCINATING FACT!

SAFER JET-PACK

SAFER stands for Simplified Aid For EVA Rescue. It works by sending out jets of nitrogen gas. There are 24 jets pointing in three different directions (up and down, backward and forward, and side to side). By choosing which jets to use, the astronaut can vary his or her direction.

BIG WORD ALERT!

NASA

The National Aeronautics and Space Administration: the organization that carries out space exploration for the USA.

GO FOR IT!

On March 5, 2005, 47 people went surfing on Australia's Gold Coast on a single surfboard measuring 39 feet long and 10 feet wide.

Tim Arfons gets around on a jet-powered barstool. The stool reached speeds of 40 mph at a raceway in Norwalk, Ohio.

In 2006, two British women, Antonia Bolingbroke-Kent and Jo Huxster, drove a three-wheel taxi, called a tuk-tuk, 11,800 miles from Thailand to England through 12 countries.

twist it!

WAY TO GO!

This bride and her bridesmaids rode to her wedding in a tractor bucket in China in 2008. The groom arrived in his own tractor bucket, also decorated with balloons.

David Smith, from Missouri, USA, used a cannon to fire himself across the US/Mexican border. He waved his passport as he flew past customs control.

Paul Stender's Port-O-Jet consists of a wooden washroom hut that is powered by a 50-year-old, 750-pound Boeing jet engine. It travels at 46 mph and throws 33-foot fireballs from the burner at the back. Paul drives it while seated on the original toilet inside.

LITTLE AND LARGE

extreme vehicles

Did you know that you can stretch a car and make it longer? Not like a rubber band—a stretch limo is a luxury car made longer by cutting it in two and putting an extra section in the middle. Whereas an ordinary car is around 15 feet long, stretch limos usually measure about 28 feet, but the world's longest is 100 ft long. However, some people think that small is beautiful. The tiniest cars are less than 4 feet high, and the most minuscule planes are just 13 feet long. That's about the same length as a car.

Driven mad

Gregory Denham from California, USA poses on his Dream Big motorcycle. Rumored to be the biggest motorcycle in the world, it stands a huge 11 feet high and 20 feet long. Denham wanted a cycle that could perform like a Monster Truck, so he went ahead and built one for himself!

ROOM FOR EVERYONE

Meet one long, long limo, made by Jay Ohrberg—known as "The King of Show Cars." This lengthy motor is 100 feet long and has a helicopter landing site at the back. Add some friends... and drive!

Room for one

The Bede BD-5J is a 13-foot-long plane, powered by a tiny jet engine with a top speed of 300 mph. With room enough for just one, it was piloted by 007 in the James Bond film *Octopussy*.

Let's compare...

The titchy Bede BD-5J with the world's biggest airliner, the Airbus A380

AIRBUS A380
A380

	Height	Length	Max weight	Wingspan	Max speed
Bede BD-5J	5.6 ft	12 ft	0.425 ton	17 ft	300 mph
Airbus A380	79 ft	239.5 ft	620 tons	262 ft	587 mph

Check out the bags of lead shot, designed to keep the nose down.

EXPERIMENTAL

For more on the Airbus A380, turn to page 40.

twist it!

Benji Ming was so enraged at the small audiences he was attracting for his shows at the Edinburgh Festival, Scotland, that he transferred his performances from the theater to the confines of a Smart car. He delivered a comic monologue to a packed house—an audience of one in the passenger seat.

Twenty-one Malaysian students crammed themselves into a Mini Cooper in June, 2006.

Jasper, a black Doberman-Labrador owned by Sir Benjamin Slade in England, travels everywhere by stretch limo.

¡EXTREME!

Streeeetch!

There's room to be creative with the interiors in this 40-foot-long Hummer, owned by Scott Demaret from Bristol, England.

SMALL IS BEAUTIFUL

Designed to seat only one person and a shopping bag, the Peel P50 was a three-wheeled micro-car, first produced in 1963. It had one door, a single windshield wiper, and only one headlight. With vital statistics of just 53 inches by 39 inches, its tiny frame weighed in at only 130 pounds, but could manage a speed of 38 mph. Handy for slipping into any confined parking space, the Peel had just one drawback—no reverse gear!

Ripley's Believe It or Not! LONDON

PEEL 50

ROBOTS ARE REAL!

man machines

The robots are coming! Robots in films are often walking, talking, machines that look like metal people. Real robots are often not quite so lifelike, but there are more than six million robots in the world today.

A million of them are industrial robots. These are computer-controlled arms that help to make things in factories. The other five million or so are service robots. These include robot toys, vacuum cleaners, and lawn mowers. Honda's ASIMO robot (see far right) is a real walking, talking robot. ASIMO is 4 feet tall and weighs 120 pounds. It can walk at 1.5 mph and even run a little faster.

20-foot flames shoot from its nostrils.

The word robot was used for the first time in a theater play called Rossum's Universal Robots by the Czech writer Karel Capek in 1921.

Mighty muncher

Its jaws crush with a force of 20,000 lb: powerful enough to bite a car in two.

Robosaurus is a 40-foot-tall robot that can lift, crush, burn, and bite. Created by American inventor Doug Malewicki, it's as high as a five-story building and is controlled by a human pilot strapped inside the monster's head. As flames jet out of its nostrils, its jaws can tear into a car, ripping it in two.

A large truck engine in the tail powers the beast.

Robosaurus weighs 29 tons.

UNREAL

Japanese engineers have developed a robotic wine taster that can tell the difference between 30 different types of grape.

Two Scottish inventors have made a robotic bird of prey to scare off pigeons. The robot falcon sounds like a real bird and can even call the owner by cell phone to warn that its battery is running low.

US government scientists have developed a tiny solar-powered robot fly that weighs less than a paper clip. Its inventors believe it could be used for spying.

The Toyota Motor Corporation built a robot that can play the violin. At its launch, the 5.5-foot-tall robot violinist played "Pomp and Circumstance," a piece of well-known music written by Edward Elgar.

>> HOW DO YOU DO? <<

This robot wants to be a real boy! The iCub acts like a human toddler, even making lots of noise: but it can be turned off when it just gets too much!

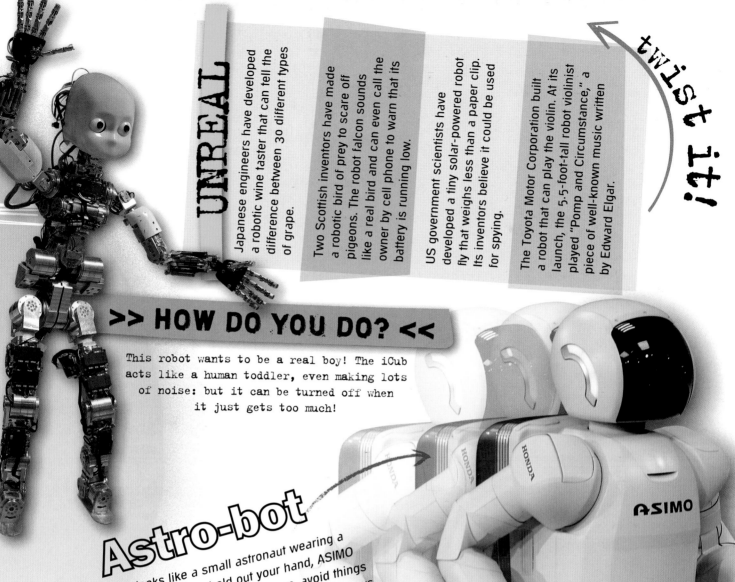

Astro-bot

Honda's ASIMO robot looks like a small astronaut wearing a backpack. It is 4 feet tall and if you hold out your hand, ASIMO gives you a handshake. It can walk, climb stairs, run, avoid things in its way, and recognize faces. It also knows when someone says its name and can answer questions. ASIMO stands for Advanced Step in Innovative MObility. When its battery is running low, the clever robot will walk to a charging station for recharging.

DOUBLE TAKE

Zou Renti, from Xi'an, China, and his twin appeared at a robotics conference in Beijing in October, 2006. However, his twin was not flesh and blood but a fully operational, robotic "clone" of himself.

FOR SAIL

If your boat doesn't have an engine, you could roll up your sleeves and row it, or you could hoist a sail and let the wind do the work.

wind power

A small boat is fun to sail, but a big racing yacht is one of the most exciting ways to travel. Racing yachts can slice through the waves at 35 mph. Super yachts more than 100 feet long can go even faster. A few of the 50,000 ships that carry goods and materials around the world have been built with sails, too. Using wind power instead of engines saves fuel.

Each mast is 164 ft tall.

The sails are made from a strong synthetic fabric and cover 27,000 square feet.

The ship can carry 308 passengers and has seven decks.

Even enormous cargo ships can be wind powered. SkySails are huge computer-controlled kites that give extra power and help to save fuel.

BELUGA PROJECTS

powered by SkySails

CLOSE TO THE WIND

The Wind Surf is a cruise liner that can be powered by either computer-controlled sails or engines. Its sails unfurl automatically from the 164-foot-tall masts within two minutes of pushing a button on the ship's bridge. Using only sails, its top speed is about 15 mph, around the same as its maximum speed on engine power.

>> PLAIN SAILING >>

French veterinarian Raphaela Le Gouvello crossed the Indian Ocean on a sailboard just 26 feet long and 4 feet wide. The 3,900-mile journey took 60 days. Raphaela spent eight hours a day at the sail. She has also crossed the Atlantic and Pacific Oceans and the Mediterranean Sea by sailboard.

The ship is 615 feet long, 66 feet wide, and weighs around 16,000 tons.

WIND SURF

WATER WAYS

Japanese sailor Kenichi Horie spent three months sailing alone across the Pacific Ocean on a yacht made from beer barrels.

British woman Hilary Lister sailed across the English Channel between England and France in August, 2005, even though she could not move her arms or legs. She steered her yacht by sucking and blowing through tubes that operated the rudder and sails.

During a round-the-world voyage in 1997, British yachtsman Tony Bullimore survived for five days underneath his capsized yacht in the icy Southern Ocean until help arrived.

When a Russian yacht lost its rudder in the Southern Ocean in 2005, the crew replaced it with a cabin door.

twist it!

BIG WORD ALERT!

CAPSIZED

Upturned. A capsized boat is one that has rolled upside-down.

Ripley explains...

Thrust

Low pressure

Sail

BOAT

Wind direction

High pressure

A yacht sail works like an aircraft wing. When a sail fills with air, it forms the same curved shape as a wing. This changes the flow of air to create low pressure. The low pressure pulls the boat along. It can move a yacht in a different direction than the wind by setting the sails at the correct angle.

Ripley's Believe It or Not!®

BRICK BOAT

It took Peter Lange from New Zealand three months to build his 20-foot-long brick boat using 676 bricks. Amazingly, it didn't sink!

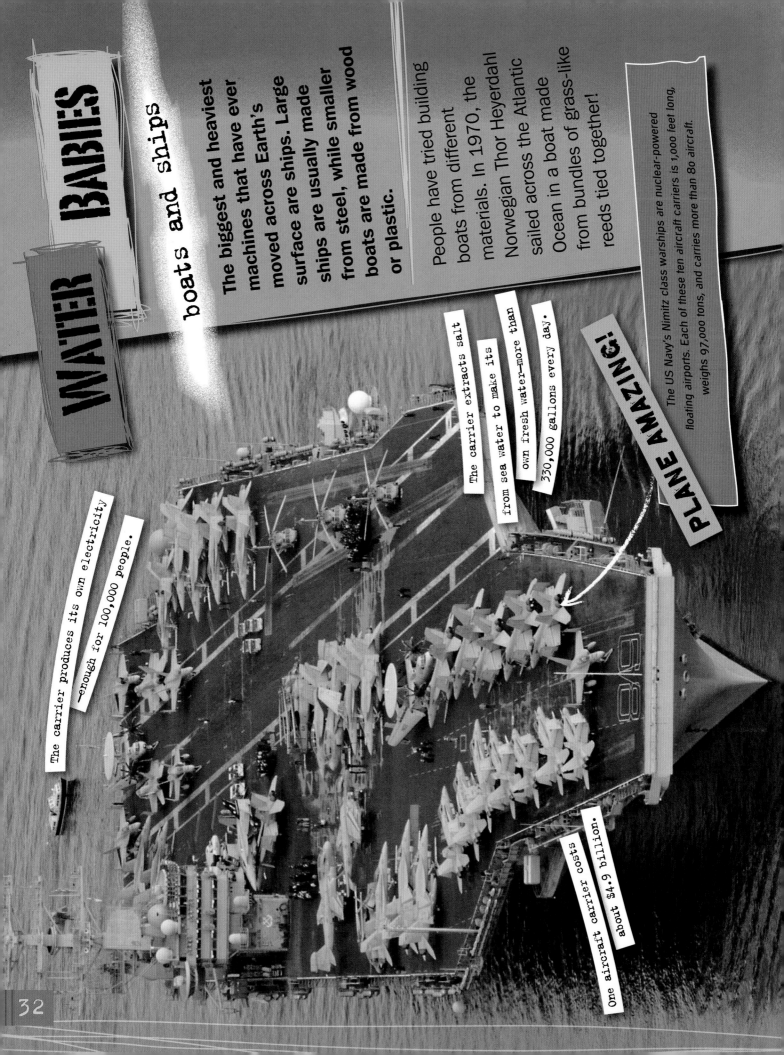

WATER BABIES

boats and ships

The biggest and heaviest machines that have ever moved across Earth's surface are ships. Large ships are usually made from steel, while smaller boats are made from wood or plastic.

People have tried building boats from different materials. In 1970, the Norwegian Thor Heyerdahl sailed across the Atlantic Ocean in a boat made from bundles of grass-like reeds tied together!

The US Navy's Nimitz class warships are nuclear-powered floating airports. Each of these ten aircraft carriers is 1,000 feet long, weighs 97,000 tons, and carries more than 80 aircraft.

The carrier produces its own electricity —enough for 100,000 people.

The carrier extracts salt from sea water to make its own fresh water—more than 330,000 gallons every day.

PLANE AMAZING!

One aircraft carrier costs about $4.9 billion.

MILK FLOAT

Inspired by the milk cartons on his breakfast table, Frank Bölter folded some Tetrapack paper (which is what cartons are often made from) and made a 30-foot-long boat. He launched it on the River Elbe in Germany in 2007.

UP AND OVER

One minute it's a ship, the next it's a floating platform for scientists at the Scripps Institute of Oceanography in San Diego, California. Most of the 350-foot-long FLIP (Floating Instrument Platform) can be flooded with water to make the stern sink and flip the bow into the air.

BY THE WAY...

During World War II, a British scientist came up with the idea of using icebergs as aircraft carriers. Although a model was built on a lake in Canada in 1943, the plan was scrapped because the ice melted too easily.

twist it!

FLOAT YOUR BOAT

In 1991, archaeologists in Egypt found a fleet of wooden boats, each 60 feet long, built nearly 5,000 years ago.

James Castrission and Justin Jones rowed their kayak 2,050 miles across the Tasman Sea between Australia and New Zealand. Their voyage took 62 days, paddling up to 18 hours a day.

In March, 2003, comedian Tim Fitzhigham rowed a kayak made of paper 160 miles down the River Thames. When it leaked during the eight-day journey, he sealed the holes with tape.

In 2003, Robert McDonald from Emmeloord in the Netherlands stayed afloat for 19 minutes in a boat made from 370,000 popsicle sticks.

A regatta held on the Mohawk River near Canajoharie, New York, involves boats made from recycled materials, including plastic milk cartons and bottles.

UP, UP, AND AWAY

balloons

Balloons and airships are actually lighter than air. They contain a gas that weighs less than the air around them. Airships are filled with helium, whereas most balloons are filled with hot air. Hot air is lighter than cold air—that's why smoke floats upward from a fire.

Airships are powered by engines and propellers, and they can be steered, but balloons drift wherever the wind blows them. Every year, more than 700 balloons take part in the world's biggest balloon festival in Albuquerque, New Mexico.

The first creatures to fly in a hot-air balloon were a rooster, a duck, and a sheep in 1783 in France.

MAN POWER

The 150-foot-long Action Man that moved through the skies over London claimed to be the world's biggest parachutist balloon.

Ripley explains...

Hot air inside balloon

Envelope

Basket

Burners

Burners above a balloon pilot's head burn propane gas from cylinders in the basket, where the pilot stands. The roaring flame heats the air above it inside the balloon's envelope. The lighter air rises and carries the balloon up with it. The pilot can turn the flame on and off to change the balloon's height above the ground.

BIG BIRD

Balloons can be built in all sorts of shapes, like this eagle. When air is heated by the balloon's gas burners, it expands and fills every part of the eagle.

A LOT OF HOT AIR

At an air base in Chambley, France, in 2005, 261 balloons lined up to float into the air at the same time.

World flight

In 1999, Bertrand Piccard and Brian Jones flew the part air-, part helium-filled Breitling Orbiter 3 balloon all the way around the world in one non-stop flight—the first time it had ever been done. The balloon took off in Switzerland, and landed in Egypt.

Helium

Hot air

Gondola

Frenchman Henri Giffard built the first airship and flew it 16 miles from Paris to Trappe on September 24, 1852.

The balloon was in the air for 19 days, 21 hours, 55 minutes and flew a total distance of 29,029 miles.

When fully inflated, the balloon stood 180 feet tall.

Propane gas fueled six burners that heated air in the balloon.

The crew traveled inside a sealed capsule, called a gondola, hanging underneath the balloon.

The gondola had flying controls and instruments at one end, a bed in the middle, and a toilet at the other end.

Winds blew the balloon along at up to 110 mph.

Ripley's —— *Believe It or Not!*®

COUCH LIFT

Kent Couch made a 200-mile flight over the state of Orgeon, USA, in 2007 while sitting on a lawn chair. The chair was held aloft by 105 balloons filled with helium. Couch reached a height of 14,000 feet and controlled his height by dropping water to go higher or popping balloons to go down. As the wind blew him toward mountains, he popped some balloons and landed in a field near Union, Oregon. The flight lasted 8 hours, 45 minutes.

105 balloons

14,000 feet!

CHAIR LIFT

Balloon pilot Pete Dalby floated over Bristol, England, sitting comfortably in an armchair hanging under a hot-air balloon!

SLOW DOWN!

parachutes

When mighty machines get going, it takes a lot of force to stop them. The fastest vehicles sometimes use parachutes to help them to slow down. The space shuttle lands at 218 mph. That's as fast as a racing car at top speed, but the space shuttle weighs a lot more, about 100 tons. To help it slow down, a huge 40-foot-wide parachute pops out of its tail. It catches so much air that it acts like a brake. Parachutes ease the speed of falling things, too.

The bigger a parachute is—the larger its surface area—the more drag it creates.

Whoa!

The space shuttle orbiter stops with a little help from air resistance, or drag.

Ripley explains...

Canopy

Cells

Lines

A simple round parachute floats straight down, slowed down by air caught underneath it. Most parachutists now use a ram-air canopy that acts a bit like a paraglider. When a ram-air canopy opens, air rushes into pockets (called cells) sewn into it. The air-filled cells give the parachute the shape of a wing. Instead of coming straight down, it flies like a glider.

HIGH FLIERS

French kitesurfer Sebastien Garat competes in the finals of the Kiteboarding World Championship in Sotavento, Fuerteventura, Spain. Using a wind-filled kite, competitors use the short time between uplift and landing to perform breathtaking acrobatics.

ground control

Safely down, and the parachutes are cut free. The Apollo 11 crew await pickup in their Command Module.

The Apollo 15 Command Module "Kitty Hawk," with astronauts David R. Scott, Alfred M. Worden, and James B. Irwin aboard, nears a safe touchdown in the mid-Pacific Ocean to end their Moon landing mission in 1971. Although it caused no harm to the crew, one of the three main parachutes failed to function properly.

Don't Let Go!

Skydiver Greg Gasson hangs by just one hand from his parachute strap, high above Eloy, Arizona.

twist it!

WHAT A DRAG

The jet-powered cars that set speed records are so fast that they use a braking parachute to slow down until they reach a speed slow enough for the car's wheel brakes to be used.

DOWNFALL

The Chinese Shenzhou spacecraft lands under a parachute big enough to park 100 cars on—12,900 square feet.

On August 16, 1960, Colonel Joseph W. Kittinger Jr jumped from a balloon at a height of 102,000 feet. He fell for 4 minutes, 36 seconds before opening his parachute, taking 13 minutes and 45 seconds in total to reach the ground.

When Shayna West of Joplin, Missouri, made a parachute jump in 2005, her main and reserve chutes both failed. She fell 10,000 feet and landed in a parking lot, breaking her pelvis, five teeth, and several bones in her face. She survived, along with the unborn baby she did not know she was carrying.

When a skydiver in Pittsburgh, USA, caught his foot on the way out of an aircraft door, he dangled from the plane for 30 minutes until it could land. He was unhurt.

Don Kellner from Hazleton, Pennsylvania, has made more than 36,000 skydives. His wife Darlene has made 13,000. They were even married in midair by a skydiving minister, Rev. Dave Sangley.

Full Speed Ahead

jet thrust

A jet engine is a big air blower. It blows out a jet of air like a hair dryer, but it blows a lot faster than any hair dryer you've ever used. Air shoots out of a jet engine more than ten times faster than a hurricane, and as hot as a blowtorch, so don't ever stand behind a jet engine!

Four of these engines can push a 500-ton airliner through the air at 560 mph. Planes aren't the only machines to be powered by jet engines. People have fitted jet engines to boats, cars, and even themselves. Jet thrust can also be supplied using water, steam, or certain gases.

ENGINE AT THE BACK

Allan Herridge has attached a Viper jet engine to the back of his Volkswagen Beetle. The car has its original 90-horsepower engine at the front, with the 2,000-pound thrust jet engine at the back. The jet engine can boost the car's speed from 80 mph to 140 mph in less than four seconds.

SOLO FLIGHT

This 300 horsepower jet pack enables the wearer to fly at up to 60 mph and perform tight turns and swoops, soar 30 feet up into the air, or hover on the spot. Shooting out two strong jets of water, which provide the thrust, a jet pack flight can last for up to 2 hours.

Sound of mind?

On October 15, 1997, British pilot Andy Green drove a jet-powered car called Thrust SSC faster than the speed of sound. He reached a speed of 763 mph.

JET PILOT

Swiss pilot Yves Rossy jumps out of a plane and flies through the air with a jet-powered wing strapped to his back. When the engines run out of fuel, he lands by parachute. On May 14, 2008, he made his first official demonstration flight, releasing himself from a plane at 8,000 feet above the Swiss Alps and using just his body position to change direction. In the following September, he flew across the English Channel in less than 10 minutes at a speed of up to 190 mph.

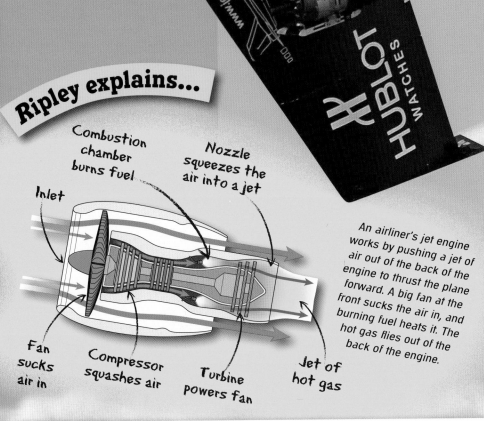

The jet engine was invented by Frank Whittle in Britain in 1930.

twist it!

Giuseppe Cannela attached a jet engine to the back of his mother-in-law's wheelchair, giving it a top speed of about 60 mph.

Paul Stender's jet-powered toilet on wheels can reach a speed of 40 mph. He races it against a jet-powered barstool.

If you're into speedy shopping, try Englishman Andy Tyler's shopping cart. It's powered by a jet engine and can speed along at more than 50 mph.

The first jet engine was a machine called the Aeolipile. It was made by Hero of Alexandria in Egypt 2,000 years ago. It was a hollow metal ball with two pipes sticking out. When water inside the ball boiled, steam sprayed out of the nozzles and made the ball spin.

CRAZY

Ripley explains...

Combustion chamber burns fuel

Nozzle squeezes the air into a jet

Inlet

Fan sucks air in

Compressor squashes air

Turbine powers fan

Jet of hot gas

An airliner's jet engine works by pushing a jet of air out of the back of the engine to thrust the plane forward. A big fan at the front sucks the air in, and burning fuel heats it. The hot gas flies out of the back of the engine.

Thrust SSC was as powerful as 1,000 family cars or 145 Formula 1 racing cars. It was powered by two jet engines from a Phantom fighter.

IN FULL FLIGHT

airliners

In 2003, Charles McKinley flew from Newark, New Jersey, to Dallas, Texas, in a crate packed in a plane's cargo hold, to save money. He was charged so much in fees and fines for doing this that he could have flown first class for the same cost!

Sit back and enjoy the view. You're in an airliner cruising through the sky 6 miles above the ground. The clouds are laid out below you like a fluffy white field. They hardly seem to be moving, but you're hurtling through the air at 560 mph, just below the speed of sound. It's sunny outside, but it's also colder than a deep freeze.

An African airline bought a Gulfstream jet for US$4.9 million on the Internet auction site eBay.

The temperature on the other side of your window could be as low as −76°F, and the air is too thin to breathe. Every year, about 12,000 airliners make more than 15 million flights, carrying over 2 billion passengers.

Its huge wings measure 262 feet from tip to tip. They're big enough to park 70 cars on them.

MIGHTY BEAST!

The Airbus A380 "super-jumbo" is the first airliner to have two passenger decks, one above the other, running the whole length of the aircraft. It made its first flight on April 27, 2005, taking off from Toulouse, France, then spending four hours circling over the Bay of Biscay while engineers carried out tests. It can carry as many as 840 passengers, although most airlines will fit about 525 seats inside it.

FLIGHT OF FANCY

Yes, this really is the inside of a plane. The Airbus A380 is more hotel than aircraft.

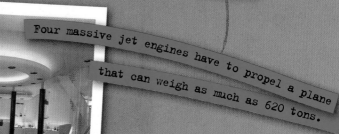

Four massive jet engines have to propel a plane that can weigh as much as 620 tons.

40

CLEARED FOR TAKEOFF

John Davis spent eight years building an exact copy of a Boeing 747 airliner cockpit in the spare bedroom of his modest home. A 6-foot screen in front of the cockpit shows views of places from the Alps to New York.

Winglets The Airbus A380 has massive wings: its wingspan is the same as the length of a football field. If the wings were the same construction as on other airliners, in order to get the massive Airbus off the ground, they would have to be incredibly long: too long for airports, which all have a maximum wingspan of just 262 feet. Designers of the Airbus A380 looked to the wings of an eagle for a solution to the problem.

Here's the science

The tip of an airliner's wing stirs up the air it is moving through. The spinning air stops the wing from working at its best, so the wing has to be made even longer. Designers noticed how an eagle's wingtips curl upward as it flies. It gave them an idea. They made turned-up wingtips, called winglets, for the A380. Each winglet blocks the spinning air and so the wingspan can be kept to 262 feet.

If five giraffes stood like a tall tower, each one on the head of the one below, they would be the same height as the new Airbus.

The two decks of the 239-foot-long aircraft cover a surface area of 5,380 sq feet, the same as ten squash courts.

Quieter. Smarter.

A380

F-WWOW

5,600 people could stand under the shelter of its wings.

Fuselage

The heavier an aircraft, the more fuel used. The Airbus A380 is longer, wider, and has more passengers than any other aircraft, but scientists constructed the outside of the aircraft from an aluminum and fiberglass blend, which is strong yet light.

IN A SPIN

vertical takeoff

Hoverflies are little flies that can stay in the same spot in midair as if hanging at the end of an invisible thread. Some aircraft can do the same thing. They can take off straight up into the air and hover in one spot. Most of them are helicopters.

Long, thin blades on top of a helicopter whirl around hundreds of times a minute, blowing air down like a big fan. The whirling blades blow hard enough to lift a helicopter weighing several tons off the ground. There are about 45,000 helicopters in service all over the world. Helicopters have saved more than 3 million lives since the first helicopter rescue in 1944.

The tips of the blades whirr around at 450 mph. The two propellers spin in opposite directions to stop the whole plane from rotating.

Refueling probe. The Osprey uses this to fill its tanks with fuel from a flying tanker-plane.

The Osprey can carry 24 passengers.

A tail fin provides stability.

MASTER STROKE

Leonardo da Vinci (1452–1519) made a sketch of a flying machine that seems to anticipate the helicopter, though it's not clear how he thought it would work.

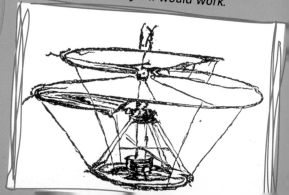

WHAT A CHOPPER! OR IS IT?

The V-22 Osprey takes off like a helicopter. Then its engines and propellers tilt forward and it flies like a plane. This means it can take off and land almost anywhere, even in remote parts of the world where there is no runway. Built for the military and perfect for use on aircraft carriers, each V-22 Osprey costs about $100 million.

The Russian Mil Mi-26 is a giant among helicopters. It can carry more than 80 people or 20 tons of cargo.

Frenchman Gustave de Ponton d'Amécourt invented the word helicopter in 1861.

A drive shaft runs through both wings, connecting rotors together, so that if one of the engines breaks down, the other engine will power both propellers.

At speeds of up to 315 mph, the V-22 Osprey flies twice as fast as a helicopter.

twist it!

brought it down!
the hovering helicopter it had been shot from, and
a tranquilizer dart near Gustavus, Alaska, charged
In March 2007, a moose that had been shot with

Mount Everest, at a height of 29,029 feet.
helicopter on top of the world's highest mountain,
In 2005, Frenchman Didier Delsalle landed his

16 years old.
to do it, because US pilots have to be at least
only 14 years of age. He had to go to Canada
and a helicopter on the same day when he was
California, made his first solo flights in a plane
In 2003, Jonathan Strickland from Inglewood,

called the Pixelito, weighing only ¼ ounce.
Alexander van de Rostyne created a tiny helicopter

¡TI NIGS

uplifting!

Helicopters usually land with ease, but this one had strongman Franz Muellner to contend with. When the 4,000-pound aircraft landed on his shoulders, he managed to hold it off the ground for nearly a minute in Vienna in 2006.

43

BLAST OFF!

rocket power

Three... two... one... lift off. If you want to be an astronaut, you'll need a rocket. It's the only way to get into space and it's the boldest, fastest journey you will ever make. The mighty *Saturn V* rocket launched astronauts on their way to the Moon. Today, rocket power takes astronauts to the International Space Station. By the end of 2008, nearly 500 people from 39 countries had hitched a ride on a rocket into space. Rockets blast satellites into orbit, too, and they send probes to the Moon and planets. Back here on Earth, smaller firework rockets light up the sky at special events and celebrations.

Ariane 5 can launch satellites weighing up to 10 tons.

Each of the two booster rockets weighs 286 tons.

Ariane 5 made its first flight in 1996.

Upper stage

ARIANE 5

eutelsat

arianespace
Service & Solutions

Payload

An Ariane 5 rocket is 170 feet high and at liftoff weighs 860 tons.

Ariane 5 rockets launch satellites for the European Space Agency (ESA). They blast off from ESA's spaceport in French Guiana, South America. Ariane 5 is massive. It stands as tall as a 14-story building and weighs as much as 600 cars. It is actually four rockets linked together. The core stage and two booster rockets fire first. When their fuel is used up, they fall away and the upper stage fires to place the cargo in orbit around Earth.

High point

SpaceShipOne rocketed into history in 2004, when it became the first private, manned spacecraft to reach a height of 62 miles. In doing this, its team members won the Ansari X Prize of $10 million in a competition to encourage civilian spaceflight.

44

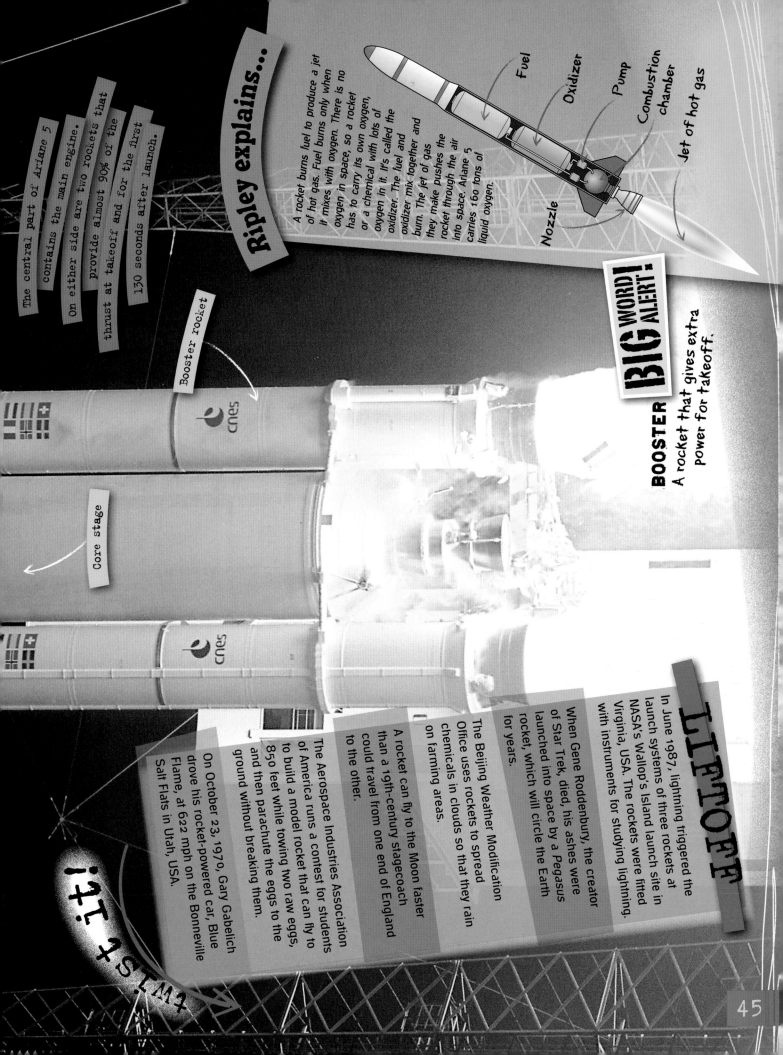

Ripley explains...

A rocket burns fuel to produce a jet of hot gas. Fuel burns only when it mixes with oxygen. There is no oxygen in space, so a rocket has to carry its own oxygen, or a chemical with lots of oxygen in it. It's called the oxidizer. The fuel and oxidizer mix together and burn. The jet of gas they make pushes the rocket through the air into space. Ariane 5 carries 160 tons of liquid oxygen.

Fuel

Oxidizer

Pump

Combustion chamber

Jet of hot gas

Nozzle

The central part of Ariane 5 contains the main engine. On either side are two rockets that provide almost 90% of the thrust at takeoff and for the first 130 seconds after launch.

Booster rocket

Core stage

BIG WORD! ALERT:

BOOSTER
A rocket that gives extra power for takeoff.

LIFTOFF

In June 1987, lightning triggered the launch systems of three rockets at NASA's Wallop's Island launch site in Virginia, USA. The rockets were fitted with instruments for studying lightning.

When Gene Roddenbury, the creator of Star Trek, died, his ashes were launched into space by a Pegasus rocket, which will circle the Earth for years.

The Beijing Weather Modification Office uses rockets to spread chemicals in clouds so that they rain on farming areas.

A rocket can fly to the Moon faster than a 19th-century stagecoach could travel from one end of England to the other.

The Aerospace Industries Association of America runs a contest for students to build a model rocket that can fly to 850 feet while towing two raw eggs, and then parachute the eggs to the ground without breaking them.

On October 23, 1970, Gary Gabelich drove his rocket-powered car, Blue Flame, at 622 mph on the Bonneville Salt Flats in Utah, USA.

Twist it!

MIGHTY MACHINES INDEX

ACKNOWLEDGMENTS

COVER (l) © Kirill Alperovich – istockphoto.com, (r) Reuters/Ali Jareki; **2** (b) Michael J. Gallagher; **3** (r) Bobby Hunt; **4** (c) Sipa Press/Rex Features; **5** (t/l) © Kirill Alperovich – istockphoto.com; **6** (b/l) Andy Wilman/Rex Features; **6–7** (sp) Photo courtesy of BigFoot 4x4, Inc. © All rights reserved, (bgd) © Eric Gevaert – istockphoto.com; **7** (t/r) Reuters/Ali Jarekji, (b/r) Mike Derer/AP/PA Photos; **8** (b) Rex Features; **8–9** (c) Rex Features; **9** (t/r) Doug Hall/Rex Features, (b) Glenn Roberts, Motorcycle Mojo Magazine/www.motorcyclemojo.com; **10** (c) Reuters/David Mercado; **11** (c) Sean Dempsey/PA Archive/PA Photos, (b) Tina Norris/Rex Features, (r) Bobby Hunt; **12** (sp) Barcroft Media; **13** (r, c/r, b/r) Barcroft Media, (t/l) Patrick Barth/Rex Features, (t/r) Rinspeed; **14** (c) Reuters/Ho New, (b/l) Reuters/Toshiyuki Aizawa; **15** (c) Greg Williams/Rex Features, (b) Joel King/Wrigley's Airwaves ®, (r) Reuters/Sebastian Derungs; **16** Reuters/Reinhard Krause; **17** (t/l) Camera Press, (l) Gavin Bernard/Barcroft Media, (t/c, t/r) Barcroft Media, (b) BP/Barcroft Media; **18** (b/l, sp) Reuters/Tim Wimborne; **19** (l) Courtesy NASA, (b) Jennifer Podis/Rex Features, (t/r) Arko Datta/AFP/Getty Images; **20** (sp) Photo © Harrod Blank; **21** (t) © Duncan Walker – istockphoto.com; **22** (c, t/r) © Bettmann/Corbis; **22–23** (b) Official ISR Photo; **23** (t, t/r) Greg Kolodziejzyk/www.human-power.com, (c/r) Reuters/Anuruddha Lokuhapuarachchi, (b/r) Reuters/Reinhard Krause; **24** (sp/r) Courtesy NASA; **25** (l) Michel Redondo/AP/PA Photos, (c) Michael.J.Gallagher, (t/r) ChinaFotoPress/Photocome/PA Photos; **26** (b/l) Built by Jay Ohrberg/www.jayohrberg.com, (c) Volker Hartmann/AFP/Getty Images; **27** (t/l, l) Copyright © 2006 by Juan Jimenez – Reprinted with permission, (r) Rex Features; **28** (sp) TSGT Joe Zuccaro/AP/PA Photos, (b/r) © John H. Clark/Corbis; **29** (t/l) WENN/Newscom, (b/l) Reuters/Jason Lee, (r) Reuters/Toshiyuki Aizawa; **30** (b/l) Copyright SkySails, (sp) Windstar Cruises; **31** (t/r) Richard Bouhet/AFP/Getty Images, (b) © Photos by Wally Hirsh, corrugated iron sails by Jeff Thomson; **32** (sp) © UPPA/Photoshot; **33** (t/l) Reuters/Christian Charisius, (sp) Bill Call, Scripps Institution of Oceanography, (b/l, b/r) GoldenStateImages.com © Randy Morse; **34** (l) Reuters/Ian Waldie, (r) Reuters/Denis Balibouse; **35** (l) Reuters/Stringer France, (c) © Fabrice Coffrini/epa/Corbis, (b/l) South West News/Rex Features, (b/r) Pete Erickson/AP/PA Photos; **36** (t) Rex Features, (b/r) © Carlos De Saa/epa/Corbis; **37** (t/l) Joe Jennings/Barcroft Media, (b) Reuters/Dan Chung, (t/c, t/r) Courtesy NASA; **38–39** (b) Michael Sohn/AP/PA Photos; **38** (r) Jetlev-flyer.com/Solent News/Rex Features, (r) Harry How/Allsport/Getty Images; **39** (c) Fabrice Coffrini/AFP/Getty Images; **40–41** (dp) Reuters/Charles Pertwee; **40** (b/l) Camera Press/David Dyson, (b/c, b/r) ©Airbus 2004 Camera Press/ED/RA; **41** (t, t/r) David Burner/Rex Features; **42** (r) Mary Evans Picture Library, (l) David Jones/PA Archive/PA Photos, (r) Gerry Bromme/AP/PA Photos; **43** (r) Vladimir Kmet/AFP/Getty Images; **44–45** (dp) ESA/CNES/Arianespace/Service Optique Video du CSG; **44** (l, r) Reuters/Mike Blake

Key: t = top, b = bottom, c = center, l = left, r = right, sp = single page, dp = double page, bgd = background

All other photos are from Ripley Entertainment Inc.

All artwork by Dynamo Design

Every attempt has been made to acknowledge correctly and contact copyright holders and we apologize in advance for any unintentional errors or omissions, which will be corrected in future editions.